Ecommerce Reimagined

Sharon Gai

Ecommerce Reimagined

Retail and Ecommerce in China

palgrave
macmillan

Sharon Gai
Hangzhou, China

ISBN 978-981-19-0002-0 ISBN 978-981-19-0003-7 (eBook)
https://doi.org/10.1007/978-981-19-0003-7

Cover illustration: tolgart/Getty Images

This Palgrave Macmillan imprint is published by the registered company Springer Nature Singapore Pte Ltd.
The registered company address is: 152 Beach Road, #21-01/04 Gateway East, Singapore 189721, Singapore

To everyone who looks forward to the future.

Acknowledgments

I want to first thank everyone who has accepted my interviews for the book. This was a product of the collective knowledge of several individuals. I have simply been the transcriber and curator of all of this information.

I have to thank Alibaba as a platform allowing me to learn beside seasoned ecommerce experts and giving me the chance to spearhead some of its newest projects. I've had many firsts during my time working here and it has definitely been the most interesting company to work for. For this, I want to thank Brian Wong who was an early employee at Alibaba to have brought me into Jack Ma's globalization program.

To all of the brands and hundreds of merchants that I have worked with along the way, thank you. You have each taught me something special about the Chinese market.

Thank you to Matthew Brennan and Kevin Shimota for guiding me in the very beginning of my journey as I wrote out my own version of the China I experienced. I think it takes waves more of pioneers like us to make the world understand China more deeply.

Thank you to Kate Pugh, my professor from Columbia, who had helped to guide me along my first writing journey.

Thank you to what we internally call the Mansion who were the initial group of people who wanted to publish something on China and tell the world about the stories that we endured.

I'm extremely grateful to the editorial team at Palgrave for guiding me along my first book. Special thanks to Ashwini Elango, Aurelia Heumader, and Jacob Dreyer. Special thanks also to Jacob who has been so helpful in introducing me to relevant people in the industry.

Finally, to my family, thank you for starting a family during a time that you did for me to be able to see the potential of what China can become and to my husband who has seen this book go from page 1 to now.

Prologue

What was *your* first impression of China? What was the scene that left a mark in your mind? Was it a trip to the Great Wall? Was it a CNN news article?

I suppose mine should have been a humble hospital somewhere in the second tier city of Dalian, Liaoning, China, where I was born. A port city, surrounded three sides by water in northeastern China, Dalian is part of the Great Dongbei, where people are mostly known for being down to earth and having a natural sense of humor. I left for Canada at a young age, so my impression of China didn't completely solidify until I came back to it again, some twenty years later, to a luxury molecular gastronomy vegetarian restaurant as part of a six-month-long interview process to work at Alibaba. And that's when I realized I was diving into a country that was completely unrecognizable to one that I had left twenty years ago.

To many, China is a mysterious country with massive economic growth. As the world's second largest economy, its total retail sales are almost on par with the total retail value in the US. For many luxury brands, China is already their largest consumer market. Its sheer population size at 1.4 billion people is more than 3 times that of the US. Most of the growth is attributed to China's rising middle class and the increase in disposable income with the biggest grower as the "Mass Affluent" earning approximately 40K USD a year.

As a business, it is only logical to look toward this market for growth as the markets of developed countries begin to flatten. But there is a lot more to China than just the numbers it represents. This is a book in which I want to turn those large numbers to real people and stories so that no matter who you are, whether a student, a professor, an entrepreneur, the CMO of a brand, you will be able to experience the market more closely. Few have had the chance to really live in the country, especially after Covid with its stringent laws in border entry, but I do hope to show you this other world through what I've learned and first-hand stories. I will take you to the Alibaba campus and show you how the world's largest shopping festival is created. I will take you to livestream rooms where they sell trips on rockets. I will share with you the latest adult toys in the format of a blind box that has taken China by storm.

I had the fortune of working in one of China's largest technology companies for almost five years. What I hope to show you is another world that you would not normally find on Google or YouTube. The internet world today is divided in two factions (if we are excluding the dark web that is). If you live in a world with regulated internet, there is the "normal world" dominated by Google, Facebook, and Netflix, and then, there is the China world dominated by Tencent, Alibaba, and Baidu. The contents generated from both worlds stay in their own lanes, without much crossover, mainly because of the firewall in China for western content to seep over and the invisible firewall of the Chinese language for the west. In speaking with many brands and entrepreneurs as they look toward breaking into China ecommerce, many have given me feedback that information on Chinese ecommerce is hard to find. Thus, in codifying the hundreds of conversations I have had with brands and entrepreneurs already, I have condensed those conversations in four easy-to-read chapters that can hopefully help you in understanding more about Tmall itself and the Chinese ecommerce ecosystem.

In this book, you will learn the basic building blocks of how to do ecommerce in China. This book will first set the scene by introducing the Chinese internet ecosystem and highlight all apps that are relevant for brands and businesses wishing to enter China as a market. Next, it will deep dive into fundamental ecommerce theories such as the Golden Triangle, the ecommerce equation, consumer profiles, merchandising, and explanation of in app and out of app marketing methods. I will then highlight trends seen recently in China such as livestreaming, blind boxes, SHEconomy, New Retail, quick commerce, and VR/AR. Finally, I will show you case studies of brands in China that have made their marks in a highly competitive direct to consumer space. I will explain how best work with the platform, how to choose a TP and share experiences from H&M and Adidas on their digital journeys in China. Though the occurrences pertain most to China, you will be able to apply these concepts to another country as you begin your digital journey.

And with that, happy reading and learning!

Hangzhou
2021

Sharon Gai

Contents

About the Author

Sharon Gai is a China-born Canadian who has had 10+ years in ecommerce, digital marketing, and branding. Immigrating at a young age to a new country where she did not speak the local language has trained her skills of adaptability and resilience as well as sparking her inner creativity where she is able to connect to both the East and the West. A Global Shaper in the China chapter of the World Economic Forum, Sharon has an Honors Bachelor's degree in International Development from McGill and a Masters in Information Management from Columbia University.

She started her career in ecommerce at a Fortune 500 systems integrator, enabling SMB's to conveniently order computer hardware online. She was then selected to be a part of the Alibaba Global Leadership Academy, a brainchild program of Jack Ma with a 0.3% acceptance rate, that hired global leaders to globalize Alibaba's internal business groups. In her tenure at Tmall, China's largest ecommerce platform, she has advised large to emerging internet-viral brands in crafting their digital marketing and online ecommerce strategy in China. She has served as the Head of Global Key Accounts in Tmall providing thought leadership in omnichannel strategies for Xiaomi, Adidas, AS Watson, P&G, and H&M. She has been the keynote speaker in 100 ecommerce and retail conferences such as Shoptalk, Ecomworld, Etail, and Ecommerce Asia with over 40,000 attendees as well as the presenter to governments and heads of states on the developments of the tech industry in China. She has appeared on CCTV, Techcrunch, Retail Asia, The Next Web, and the

Singularity University and enjoys sharing with the world the latest trends from China. She is the author of the book, Ecommerce Reimagined: what we can learn in retail and ecommerce from China to be released in June 2022.

CHAPTER 1

Setting the Scene

The Very Beginning

I had taken this photo when I first arrived in China to begin my Alibaba journey. I took part in a leadership development program and as part

S. Gai, *Ecommerce Reimagined*,
https://doi.org/10.1007/978-981-19-0003-7_1

of a scavenger hunt, we had to go to the location of Jack's first apartment, where Alibaba was started. If you've picked up this book, likely you will have already known some things about Alibaba as a company and its founder Jack Ma. I won't provide exigent detail on the beginning stages of the company since there are many other books that has told this story in great detail such as Duncan Clark's *The House that Jack Ma Built* and Porter Erisman's movie *Crocodile in the Yangtze*.

But in case you don't know the full story, here is the shortened version. Jack learned English while taking tourists around West Lake, grabbing every chance he could to take foreigners around. You can understand West Lake as the equivalent of Central Park in New York, a landmark in the city surrounded by bustling streets and tourist activity. Naturally, it was easy for Jack to meet a decent number of foreigners there. He publicly states that he had applied in various jobs in the past, from KFC, to the police, to being a security guard, all to be rejected at all of them.

One time, Jack was on a trip in Seattle, he searched the internet for German beer, and was left with many results. He then searched for Chinese beer, leading to no results. He then searched for anything related to China, again there were no results. He realized that China and Chinese things were basically inexistent on the internet. That was when he decided to bring China online.

A teacher at the time, he selected 18 of his students, and spent 6 months in the apartment located in the photo above that led to the Alibaba we know today.

From B2B to C2C to B2C

Alibaba.Com

The first internationally-renown product from Alibaba is Alibaba.com, a product still running today, that brought online Chinese factories.

At the time, few trusted the internet. Few had even heard of what the internet can do. Thus, the first series of employees that were hired were pivotal to the development of the company. Many books and movies have documented the group called the Iron Soldiers. These were the first set of sales agents who converted each factory to be anchor tenants on the platform. They were said to be chased down by dogs while running around rural China to onboard factories to the platform.

Today, this website is still visited by suppliers, buyers, and brands from around the world to source from factories in China.

Taobao

As Alibaba.com took flight, Jack then had the next idea of opening up Taobao as a service. The first listings were simply idle items from employees' homes of things they no longer needed. To test user experience, he had employees buy each other's goods on the platform, creating the illusion that one can make money from the platform. As other users grew, the first C2C consumer facing app was born to facilitate the buying and selling of goods among consumers.

Pretty soon, local brands started joining the platform as well as global brands shortly after that. When the team later realized that this platform can also become an advertising channel, they launched Taobao Mall.

Taobao Mall later became the Tmall that most Chinese people know today.

Tmall

Tmall was started in 2012, eight years after the formal launch of Taobao. When the team at Taobao noticed that certain brands had been able to make money on Taobao, many brands were attracted to the amount of traffic the platform offered. In the first days of ecommerce in China, most brands, like many in the US, still had their own websites as a portal for ecommerce. Because few brands were selling on the platform, the first set of brands were able to thrive in the amount of traffic. You'll learn in Chapter 4 the decision-making process that Swedish fashion house H&M had to go through to decide whether to migrate to a marketplace after spending a large amount of money in building their own ecommerce website.

The first brands that joined Tmall established a wave of success. Bestseller Group, a Danish company that set their sight on China early on, opened their first set of brands on the platform, Only, Vero Moda, and Jack Jones, that led to its success in offline stores.

This was the ad from the first Double 11 that the platform had hosted. Many of the below brands have become huge fast fashion houses in China today.

Photo of the first Taobao Mall ad for Double 11

Work, Live, Meet at Ali—Alibaba Breakdown

Alibaba today is now a digital ecosystem, one that strives to become the world's fifth largest economy. Internally, each app is called a "Business Group". For instance, Taobao is a BG or Fliggy, is a BG. Other than the consumer-facing apps that Alibaba has, few people actually know about the other BG's and industries that Alibaba plays in.

Alibaba Investor Report 2020

To understand the company, we can carve up its businesses in five main sections. The first is the **Commerce** pillar which houses the well-known consumer-facing logos of Taobao and Tmall, what Alibaba is most famous for in the eyes of the Chinese consumer. Jack had developed the term called "New Retail" in 2016, predicting that this was going to be the future of retail. Thus, Alibaba began to invest more heavily into offline retailers. Hema is a hybrid offline and online grocery market known only to Chinese consumers at the time of writing. Alibaba has also made investments in vertically integrated retailers such as Suning and Sunart. In wholesale ecommerce, there is Alibaba.com which is a website that many suppliers and brand owners might know.

In **Consumer Services**, there is Koubei and Eleme, two apps very similar to the Yelps of the world and Doordash in food delivery. Fliggy is an app that is similar to Kayak.com or Expedia.

A couple of years ago, Jack also invigorated a double H strategy called Health and Happiness, alluding that in the future, these would be the most important strategic directions the company should manage. This accounts for the many acquisitions in the entertainment sector that now includes Alibaba Pictures, Youku, Tudou and Alisports that make up the **Digital Media and Entertainment** pillar.

Finally there are other apps that are part of the **Strategic Initiatives** pillar called Dingtalk, Amap, and Tmall Genie. Dingtalk takes its liking most to Slack, a messaging service that is meant to replace email among colleagues. For those who have worked with Alibaba in some capacity in the past, you were probably mandated to download this app just to communicate with Alibaba employees. Amap is a maps service similar to Google Maps. It opened a ride hailing service in 2018. Tmall Genie is similar to the Amazon Echo, a hardware business with a voice assistant that extends into the IOT of the home.

Finally, in the **Infrastructure** pillar, we have Cainiao, Alipay and Alicloud. All of the financial transactions that are needed within the company is run by Alipay, whether it is a B2B, C2C or B2C transaction. Alipay overtook PayPal as the world's largest mobile payment platform in 2013. All of the apps also run on the cloud, which is powered by Alicloud. What originally started as an in house data center eventually was carved out to serve external customers in China and around the world. Currently it is the cloud provider with the largest market in China.

Ecommerce, an Evolution

Ecommerce in China wasn't always dominated by Tmall. When foreign brands arrived in China, most of them started websites just as they did back home. But because Taobao amassed more traffic, brands began to wonder whether it was a good idea to open shop on Tmall instead. This created a network effect. Once one anchor brand (for example Nike opened on Tmall) others followed suit. This made the consumer more invested in the platform since it's much easier to buy from one single platform than five or six disparate platforms. The strong became stronger, which leads to the gargantuan platform we have today that covers the majority of the market share in China with 290,000 brands participating in the platform.

Setting up shop in Tmall is similar to setting up shop in Amazon or opening Shopify. Brands have a back-end product to directly reach consumers. For many overseas brands, this has now become their main market entry strategy when it comes to China.

Today, this is the home page of the Taobao app.

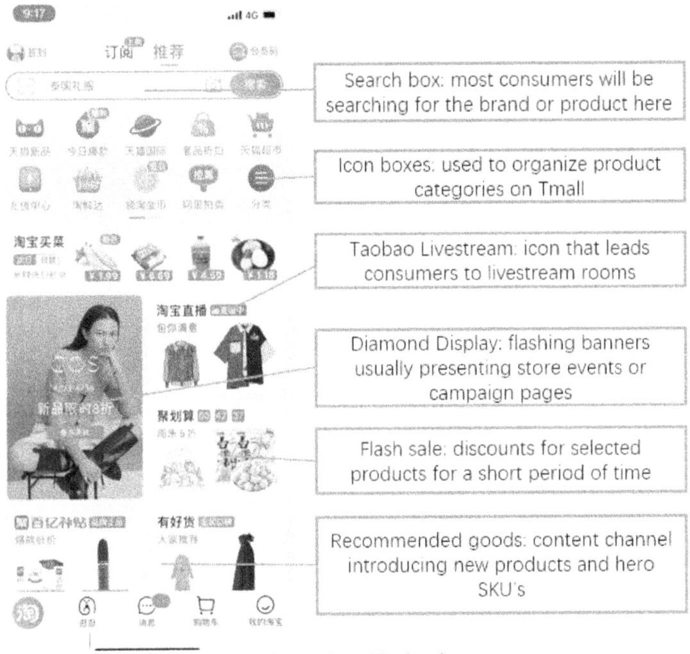

Screenshot of Taobao home page

Since Taobao is so well known amongst consumers, with around 900 million users, it is now being used as a central entrance for users to access other services such as Tmall Supermarket, Tmall Global, Fliggy's ticketing service, Eleme's good delivery or even charging money for your cell phone. This is in the Icon section as described by the above graphic. It also serves as the major source of advertising for brands that wish to advertise within the app.

The ABC's of a Tmall Store

Now that you are in Taobao, how do you display products to your consumers? This is done via a Tmall flagship store.

As an example, this is the page of Kim Kardashian's KKW Fragrance store which was opened two years ago. This is the user interface that users will interact with after they have searched something in the app to then land on a store. A standard layout is a brand display of promotional activities or brand story up top, coupons in the middle for customers to obtain discounts within the store and more items on the bottom. Several beauty brands also have quite complicated games to play to gain interaction with its fans or an Augmented Reality mirror for customers to try on certain colors. Some stores will also add a special placement for Members of the store.

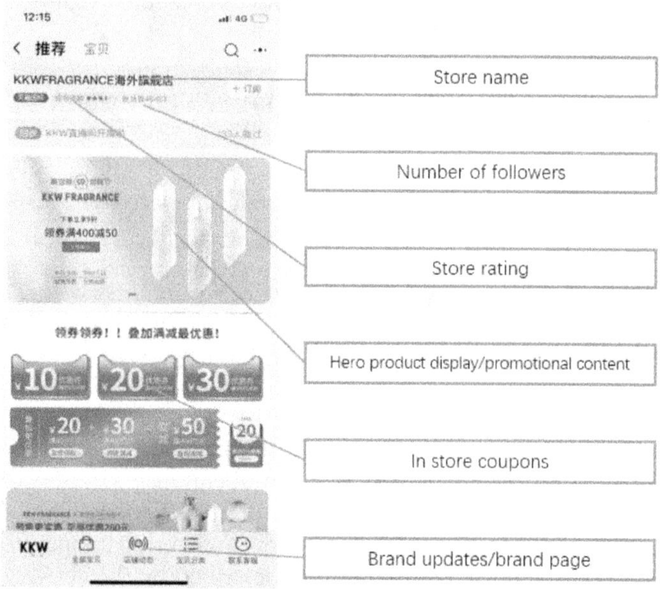

Taobao screenshot of Kim Kardashian's Flagship store

Types of Stores

The most common type of store opened is called the **Brand Flagship store**, where the Tmall team will check if you are the owner of the brand. If you are a distributor, and you wish to sell a certain brand, you will have to then obtain the rights to distribute this brand from the brand owner. Afterwards, only items from this brand will be available in this store. Unless you have a large brand to promote, or a decent number of

SKU's, I would not recommend going this route if you were starting out on the platform.

Another type of store is the **Multi-brand store**, in which, you guessed it, allows you to sell multiple brands. Supermarkets will tend to open these stores such as Costco, Kroger, or Aldi. This also means you have to have the permission to sell all of these brands in your store. However, at the time of writing, these stores are rather hard to open and requires an invitation from the platform to open one. A common multi-brand that the Tmall Food team has opened before for instance, is a multi-brand store opened by a certain government such as the Italian Pavilion or the Malaysian Pavilion.

As an alternative for smaller brands, instead of opening a flagship store, you can also join an existing Multi-brand store as well. This is a market entry strategy that has been in place for a while. In exchange for a small listing fee paid to the owner of the multi-brand store, a single brand can utilize an existing store to open itself to the Chinese market.

Next there are **Distributor stores** and **Specialty stores,** which can carry numerous brands, but will require the same levels of approval from the brand.

Celebrities have also been interested in opening something that is in their name. For instance, Kim Kardashian had opened her Tmall Global store to sell her perfume.

Taobao screenshot of Kim Kardashian's Flagship store

Billie Eilish has also done something similar to promote her new record and clothing line. The platform is also very interested in having these type of celebrity stores because of the amount of traffic that it can generate.

Taobao screenshot of Billie Eilish's Flagship store

Different Models

Beyond opening a standalone store however, there are other ways to work with the platform. The most common way is to directly open a flagship store on the platform. But there are also other ways to existing on the platform.

Tmall Classic vs Tmall Global: If you are a foreign brand, it is possible to exist in the platform as a Tmall Classic store you have already imported the brand into the country or Tmall Global, if you have not officially imported the brand into the country. Tmall Global allows products to be held in a bonded warehouse either in the local country or in China.

Tmall Direct Import: sometimes the purchasing team of Tmall Global will seek to purchase products directly because they see the potential of the product. Tmall Direct Import or TDI for short will allow the brand to use TDI as a distributor when heading into China.

Tmall Overseas Fulfillment: a program in which the product is still overseas. This service is similar to Shipbob, Floship or Locad, in which the product is put temporarily in a warehouse controlled by Cainiao. When there is an order from the side of the Chinese consumer, the brand would then ship the item.

Tmall Supermarket: is a direct purchase model in which the platform will directly purchase your goods at a discount and place your product in the Tmall Supermarket store.

Hema: is another popular direct purchase model. Hema is a brick-and-mortar supermarket in China that is mainly in Tier 1 and 2 cities. It's the epitome of new retail in China, a term that Jack had coined in 2016 as omnichannel began to heat up in China. It purports to deliver within 30 minutes within any establishment that is within a 3 km radius.

Beyond CPG Products

Tmall today has also evolved beyond simply selling small physical goods. Because most of the online traffic is in Tmall, brands also see this platform as an advertising channel. Take luxury items as an example, something that one would rather visit an offline store to purchase because of its expensive price. During Covid however in Jan 2020, Cartier opened their flagship store to see massive success in the number of people browsing their items. Today they are in the top 10 for Jewelry in the platform even though they have a very high product sales price.

Restaurants have also taken advantage of the platform as a place to extend to new customers or maintain a relationship with their offline customers. Explained in more detail in the chapter in New Retail in Chapter 3, restaurants are selling coupons and membership cards in Tmall that a user can collect and then use in an offline location.

Hotels and other experience companies have also opened shop on Tmall to sell trips to extravagant destinations.

Car companies such as Tesla, Xpeng and Volvo have all opened shop. When I was in Tmall Global, we had also sold a yacht during a Double 11 promotional event that cost millions of RMB. Recently, Tmall has also opened a division that caters to the house-buying frenzy in the Chinese market. I did see once an island being listed as an item!

The Differences Between East and West

As Amazon, another global ecommerce player, strives to expand its footprint, people often wonder what the similarities between the two platforms are. I would highlight five major differences.

Content

The first major difference would be the amount of content on Tmall versus something like Amazon. While Amazon wants its consumer to find its product quickly and efficiently, almost like running an errand, Tmall strives to have the customer stay in the app as long as possible. Thus, the hook to do this is by expanding on its content channels.

To delve deeper within this difference, Taobao has four streams of content:

1. **User generated content:** each user is encouraged to provide reviews of the product after it has been delivered. In exchange, users can obtain Taobao points which are then used to obtain further discounts. Much of the reviews now are generated with video content instead of simply text which enriches engagement on the app.
2. **KOL generated content:** Because the platform works with a set of KOLs who will also bring traffic to the platform, they also have their own pages to update content.
3. **Brand generated content:** Brands will have brand pages where they can update their own content. Store pages is also a space in which they can update information on their brand story or products.
4. **Platform generated content:** Because there are different promotional events or campaigns, the platform also generates a considerable amount of content for its users.

Focus on Brands Instead of Products

While Amazon focuses on the SKU level and getting the best price point to the customer, Tmall focuses on the brand, getting the right brand to the customer. Because Tmall's main revenue source is advertising from its merchants and brands, it is in Tmall's interest to have its consumer buy from as many brands as possible. Thus, it is also in Tmall's interest to show you different types of brands that it thinks you would like. As a consumer then, you will be shown many different brands in its "We think you will like this" stream. More explanation on this below.

A Focus on just Being the Platform

While Amazon's seemingly goal is to be a one-stop-shop for the brand, such as logistics, inventory management and store front, Tmall is mostly interested in only being the platform that enables the brand to build their own infrastructure. The Amazon equivalent is more similar to what JD is doing. Though a business model exists in which Tmall will do the purchasing, storage and management of the goods, this is more in the way of a direct purchase model in which the brands are no longer directly in touch with its consumers. The brand also does not have access to the data related to its users if it is done this way. For instance, brands can choose to directly sell to Tmall Supermarket. However, Tmall Supermarket will not be sharing additional data to the brand regarding what type of consumer is interested in the brand. Instead, Tmall mainly seeks to be the connector to link up an interested buyer to a brand.

Co-Opetition

When I had first joined Alibaba, several western colleagues found it absurd that we would onboard competitor retailers onto the platform. For instance, in the US, a retailer's ecommerce site is meant to function independently to platforms. However, in Asia and China, one will often find supermarket ecommerce websites or even websites such as Sephora be integrated within a platform.

Personalization

This piece is not something unique to Tmall. However, what Tmall does is taking it to the extreme. Also known as the Recommended section in Amazon, 猜你喜欢 cāi nǐ xǐ huān is also translated to "We think you will like this". The stream is located just below all the permanent product pieces of the app.

Perhaps the most important success factor to Taobao is the algorithm that runs beneath the surface. Most say this is a "black box" And many engineers have tried to guess the underpinnings and logic of the algorithm but few have completely been able to breakdown the logic. At the core, it's this. After a new user has logged in, and added a phone number, the app already knows some basic information of the user: where they are located and maybe some pieces of data such as income from integrating with Alipay. Next, every click the user provides, "save product", favorite, add-to-cart, purchase, repurchase or return are all actions recorded by the platform. Based on these pieces of information, the app will then reserve certain products that the user has saved or liked as re-exposure. Thus there is a concept called 千人前面 qiān rén qián miàn which means a thousand faces for a thousand people. The "face" means how the app is displayed. Because you and I will have different reactions to all of these items, our home pages will be entirely different, both pages just catered to us.

In 2019, another concept was introduced called 万人万面 wàn rén wàn miàn, or ten thousand faces for ten thousand people. This basically adds in other factors such as place and time. For instance, when you are at work, and you are looking at the P&G store, perhaps what is displayed are some office snacks. When you are at home, perhaps what is displayed are some shampoo products. The miniscule differentiation ultimately leads to more fine-tuned display of products adding to the personalization catered to the user.

Flagship 2.0, a function that was introduced in the last couple of years means to change the look of a store from day to night or depending on location of the person. For instance, when you are looking at a beauty brand in the morning, maybe they will display foundation, because there is a greater need for the user to use foundation in the morning. At night, perhaps, the store will display face masks, as that is usually an item that people use before they go to bed. Or a store front can adjust itself depending on who is viewing the store. To go back to the P&G example, if I were looking at the store, perhaps what is displayed are their top selling woman's products. If my husband were to do look at the same store, he might be viewing their top selling men's products.

The crux of continuously perfecting this algorithm is that everyone will always be looking at a personalized version of app, specific to this person's needs, instead of providing all users with one standard product. This will carry over during a campaign, where all products displayed are products that the platform thinks I have an interest in. Take this screenshot for example. All products displayed here were products that I had searched for before.

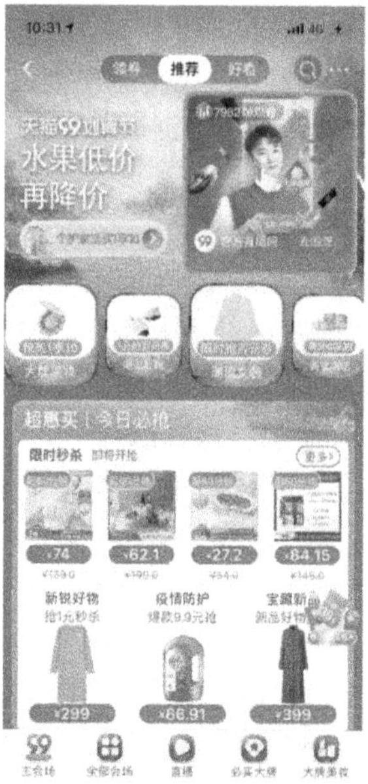

Screenshot of Taobao during its 99 campaign

This means that every campaign that is displayed contains products that are relevant to me. This leads to an increase in conversion by a huge amount versus displaying the same products to everyone in the platform.

A Different Ecosystem

Facebook, Instagram, Twitter. When I moved to China, I put these apps into a special folder in my phone called, "For Future Use". In 2009, when China wanted to grow its own set of apps, they began to restrict the usage of these western communication apps. In 2010, Google decided to leave China. This was the first breakage for home grown apps to be designed and flourish. Before I delve into the main apps for ecommerce, I do need to introduce each of these important apps in order from most ubiquitous to least.

In the west there are the FAANG companies. (I guess it is MAANG from now on since Facebook has completely thrown itself in the Meta world.) In China there is BAT—Baidu, Alibaba, Tencent, though

Bytedance, Xiaomi and companies such as Meituan are growing in importance.

By introducing each important app one by one, I hope to show readers the difference in UX and UI of consumers' favorite apps. It is also good to note the type of online user behavior as you begin to design the way you wish to face Chinese consumers. This is also a basic lesson to all brands and companies in their market entry strategy for China. This ecosystem is what makes the Chinese internet so different from a western one, also making it difficult for a brand to instantly flourish in China.

Social Apps

The next apps are pivotal in the Chinese app ecosystem. Similar to the Instagrams, Twitters and Tik Toks, these apps are the main sources of traffic and thus channels for advertising for brands.

Wechat:

Perhaps many books and online articles have spoken about Wechat and its parent company, Tencent. Few have been able to explain to its readers its significance. Advertising on Wechat is pivotal because of its omnipresence on Chinese cell phones. To show you how a brand would advertise here, I probably need to take you through the app.

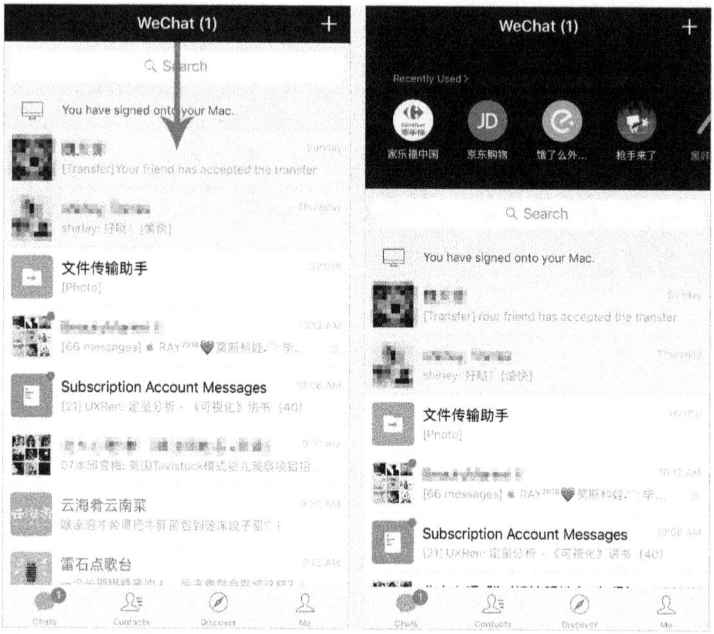

Wechat screenshot from the Nielsen Norman Group displaying mini programs
https://www.nngroup.com/articles/wechat-mini-programs/

You'll see different chat groups, such as one for colleagues, one for casual chatting with friends, one for buying houses. WeChat is an interesting tool because of the way it blends the formal work world and casual world, binding two spheres into one. If you were to open the Screen Time app in a Chinese person's phone, the first one to appear will probably be WeChat. For this reason, brands are very attracted in advertising here.

WeChat has a Friend's Circle function, similar to the Discover page that is default on Facebook's home page that allows a user to browse through the latest posts that people they have friended will send. The sentiment of users here is a state of discovery, as they scroll through, with some curiosity and nonchalance. Ads will appear here masked also as a post, to provide a seamless experience to the user. It almost seems like the brand is just another one of the user's "friends".

Mini programs is especially an important function in WeChat that becomes a seamless experience for the user to glide from a private sphere of messaging to a public sphere of the World Wide Web. From the pull down menu shown above, the circular icons are the Mini Programs from other brands, in turn serving like a website. This is how China essentially "Googles" because this WeChat search bar almost becomes a search tool.

I was in Sweetgreen on a September afternoon in Boston in 2021. It was around lunch time, and students from the surrounding school of MIT started pouring in for lunch. The line got longer and longer, at the same time food orders started picking up. I saw a sign that said to avoid standing and waiting in lines, you can download the Sweetgreen app. So I searched in the App Store and began the download. However, the app was so large, added with a weak internet, before the app finished downloading, I was already at the front of the line.

If I were to walk into a KFC or McDonalds in China, however, things might be a little different. There are usually QR codes to scan at the counter, which immediately transfers the user to the mini-program of the brand. A mini program is embedded inside WeChat, reachable via a pull down menu. Without needing to download an additional app, a user can explore inside a mini program as if it is a website. However, it is optimized for a mobile experience. Brands, especially large ones, or ones with many physical locations, will opt to create a mini program because there will be enough of its loyal customers to actively search for this brand.

Little Red Book

Home page of Little Red Book

The next notable player is Little Red Book, an app that is a mix between Instagram and Tik Tok, with a heavy user base of females born after 1990. The app is driven by the large amount of User Generated Content by its users. In its early days, there was someone called 薯队长 shǔ duì zhǎng, or the app's content curator. It acted like a community curator or a content moderator if you will. It would write articles as well as comment on other people's posts, also facilitate open groups that eventually led to the stickiness and sense of community on the app.

If you are a brand or company aiming to attract the female audience in China, I heavily suggest you in looking at Little Red Book. I also want to introduce a colloquial term here and that is 白富美bái fù měi, meaning "white, rich, and beautiful". Unlike what is societally considered "beautiful" in the west—someone who is more tanned—"being white" is a huge plus for female consumers. So this term is used to describe a group of women whose ambitions are to become those three adjectives. As unfortunate as it is perhaps, brands will target these types of influencers because they define the standard of beauty in China at the moment. However, this is also quickly changing as the Gen Z population in China is beginning to redefine the standards of beauty and curate more niche followings. You can read into Perfect Diary's case study on this in Chapter 4.

I would say Little Red Book is one of the most key marketing channels for brands who do not have any brand name established in China. Very quickly, through the employment of several KOL's on the app, an unknown brand is able, through association, to reach a wide audience and establish the "feel" of the brand based on the KOLs chosen. By placing a search bar in the app, a brand is able to direct viewers to the Tmall flagship store to complete the purchase.

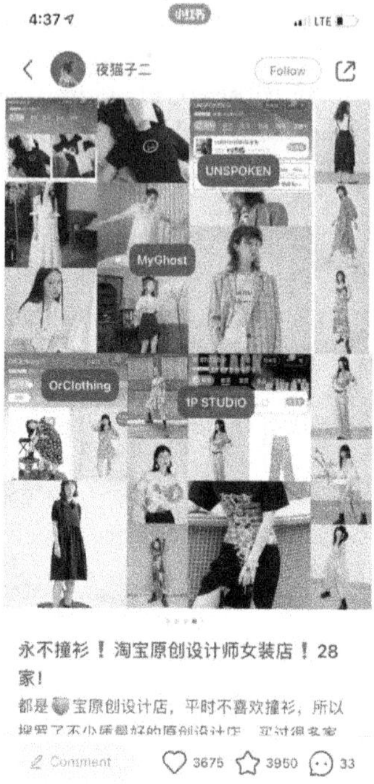

A KOL's post on LRB

The next photo is the original page of this LRB user. She has 7000 followers. Similar to Instagram, when she posts, all of her followers will receive a notification on the information she has just sent.

A KOL's home page on LRB

The route from discovery to purchase is most brands will advertise and then screenshot their Tmall store to prompt the user to go to the relevant Tmall store to find the item. Will this result in a loss in traffic? Absolutely. Search traffic is also hard to trace back to the advertising done on LRB. But there is a walled garden phenomenon happening with the apps in China which you will read about later on in the chapter that does not allow Tmall to directly insert its store link to a post.

Now, you might wonder, if LRB has much of the eyeballs, yet is still willing to direct users to Taobao, why would they not develop its own ecommerce system? Well, similar to Instagram shopping that was introduced a few years ago to have consumers more conveniently discover brands within the app and shop directly in the app, it is definitely not surprising that LRB has its own ecommerce platform also, although not so much developed as Tmall's. In fact, you will later notice that all content-heavy apps in China eventually will think of monetization in the way of ecommerce.

Douyin

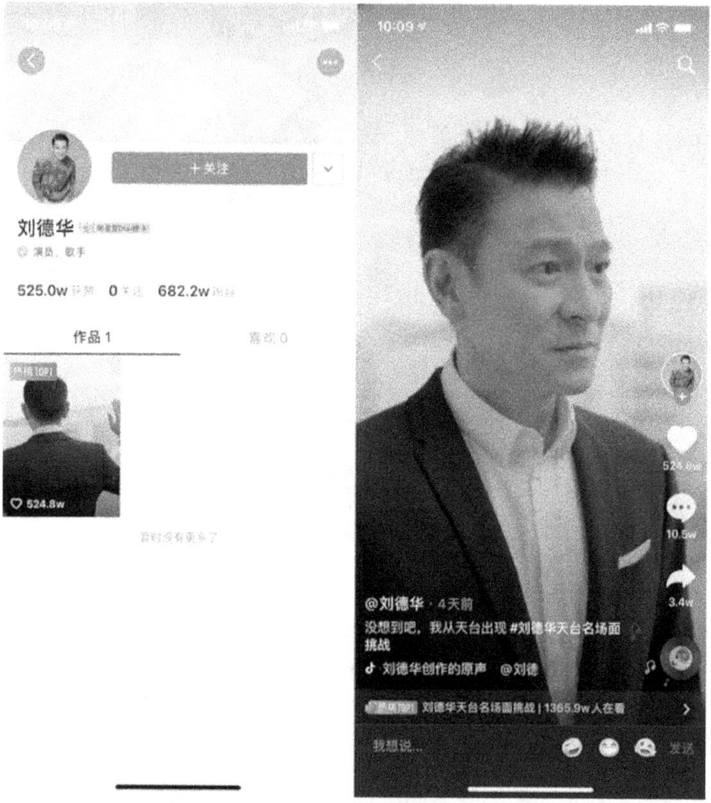

Andy Lau's profile page on Douyin

TikTok currently has over 2 billion downloads worldwide, recently passing in rank over Youtube. Its mother brand, Douyin, is the equivalent in China, virtually unheard of in the west. The app originally was meant for users to upload lip-syncing videos similar to the functions of Musical.ly. Mother company, Bytedance, later purchased Musical.ly for 1 billion USD and merged it with Douyin. As Douyin opened the livestream feature to its Chinese audience, short videos by anchor KOLs began to circulate on the internet which contributed to the growing success of Douyin in China. Today, it is the most watched platform for short video form entertainment.

Recently, Douyin has been more and more interested in growing its celebrity pages as a means to draw more users to stay in the app. Pictured above is Andy Lau's fanpage. When his page opened on the app, he shot tens of shorter bite-sized videos to then do a launch with a livestreamed interview. There was a record number of people who tuned in on this channel for his livestream.

Perhaps Douyin's biggest blessing and rise to ubiquity was during Covid, when everyone was stuck at home. Over Chinese New Year's 2020 when consumers couldn't leave their homes, a movie that was supposed to be shown in theatres brokered a deal with Douyin instead to be aired in this app which really cemented this app as a source of entertainment during that time.

Over the past two years, Douyin has been seeking to grow their ecommerce footprint. It is only natural that once you've amassed enough traffic that the next step is to monetize this traffic in the format of an ecommerce platform. To date, Douyin has established similar events such as Super Brand Days and campaign days that are different from Tmall's set calendar days.

Kuaishou

Kuai is a direct competitor to Douyin. Also in the works of building its ecommerce department, Kuai is more popular in the Tier 3 to Tier 7 cities. Cities are tier-ed in China based on economic development and population. A deeper explanation of this is provided in Chapter 2. The most commonly known cities such as Shanghai, Beijing, Shenzhen are Tier 1 cities. Tier 3 cities are simply smaller cities and extending into the countryside. A lot of videos on Kuai are rather rural-based in terms of environment. Livestreams will reflect a similar environment. Though this might be foreign visually to modern consumers, China still has roughly 50% of its population residing in rural areas which means this is still a huge demographic that this app has chosen to capture.

Screenshot of a user's profile on Kuaishou

Bilibili

Another notable content app specifically for the Gen Z space is Bilibili. This is perhaps the app that is most similar to Youtube with creators, each exhibiting their own styles to attract their niche audiences. With roughly 50 million users, 75% of them are under the age of 24, Bilibili mainly started with anime as its biggest attractor or 二次元 Èr cìyuán in Chinese. This group of consumers are highly interested in animated visuals and things that are pretty *kawaii* or cute, a phenomenon largely present in Asian consumers but quickly growing in the west as well.

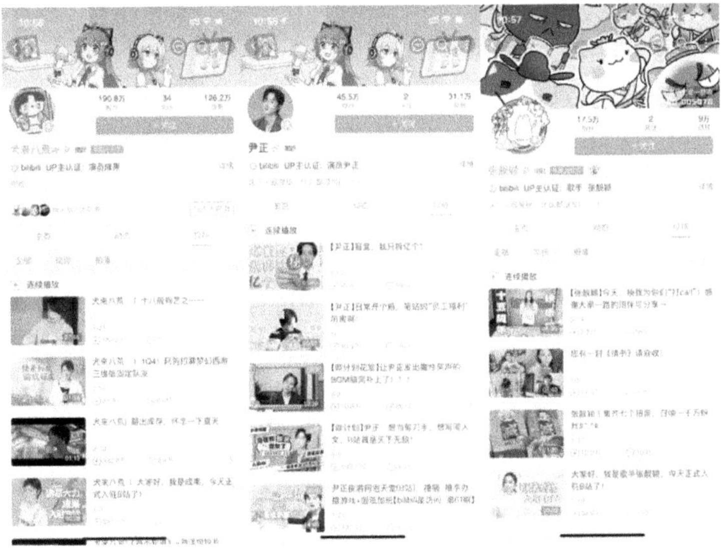

Screenshot of three Bilibili user's main page

One important thing I must note here is the way these videos are watched, something that is highly different from the west. Chinese consumers like to open something called 弹幕 dàn mù or comments from other users. I see the biggest similarity between this and Soundcloud in which users can pause at a certain time of the song and write comments that other users can then see. Just imagine watching Squid Game on Netflix and there are flying commentary from other users across the screen at all times. Where would your eyeballs even focus?! Below is a photo to show as an example, where the words in white are comments that are left by other users.

Screenshot of a Bilibili video with Danmu

I must confess, at first, I wasn't used to this way to consuming content. But now that I have turned this function on, it is hard for me to turn off. I've noticed that the flying comments actually enrich the show in a huge way. If there were originally plot twists or ambiguous scenes, the comments begin to act as a guide. This is also similar to watching two trains of thoughts at the same time and requires a tiny bit of multi-tasking. The main show is the video I am watching, but in the background, it's interesting to see the train of thought collected from the other thousands of viewers. It's a strange feeling of togetherness that is absent on Netflix or Youtube.

Zhihu

The equivalent of Quora is called Zhihu in China, a question and answer system that has amassed up to 220 million users by the end of 2018. Because of the intractability of the site, many brands have now found ways to advertise in the app such as the one below.

Similar to most social networks, user registration was invitation-only in the beginning. This strategy was to ensure high quality of questions, as well as hosting professional questions and answers.

Screenshot from Zhihu

Alright! Have we confused you enough yet with the different types of apps that a consumer uses on a daily basis? The important thing to note here is simply the different channels of marketing available for your brand. You will see these apps repeated in Chapter 2 when we are talking about the AIPL model. Now onto the apps that are more related to brands.

Pinduoduo

Home page of Pinduoduo

A notable ecommerce app is Pinduoduo, started in 2015 by ex-Googler Colin Huang. Using social commerce has the main tool of differentiation, PDD was able to have its users send their order to friends on social media. If other users would join in the purchase, the price of the item would go down. This function allowed its users to spread its purchases and invite other users to join the platform for a very low cost, which paved the way for its huge number of users today.

Mostly marketed to consumers in Tier 3 to 7 cities, PDD appeals to a different segment versus Taobao, which is more used by consumers in Tier 1 and 2 cities. Recently it has also seen a change in branding with an agri-tech focus where a huge concentration is put on connecting farmers to consumers as well as a bigger C2M push in which consumers have direct access to manufacturers.

Pinduoduo has seen its merchant base expand rapidly to reach 8.6 million active merchants within 6 years of its founding. Though this is a fast-growing ecommerce channel in China, it is still relatively small in total market share. Because most products are also quite inexpensive, most global brands stay away from opening flagship stores in this platform. However, as the daily active user count start rising in the app, it is not impossible that more and more brands will join the platform.

JD

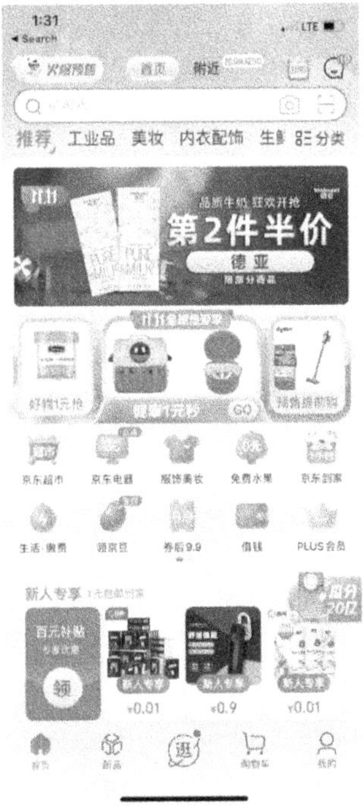

Home page of JD

A final player is JD who got its claim to fame from fast delivery and owning its own logistics. Second to Taobao in terms of market share, JD is again different from Taobao in terms of strength in product categories. While Tmall is more well-versed in the fashion world, JD got its name from mostly selling electronics, mobile phones, and computers. A large portion of its sales are from JD Direct Purchase in which the platform directly purchases the product from the consumer and facilitates the product in its warehouse. Thus, JD is known for speed in delivery compared to Tmall in which most brands will host its own logistics. The platform then has less control on delivery times. Colloquially it is known in China to order from JD if a user needs something delivered quickly.

Choosing the Right Ecommerce Platform

Now that you have learned about all of the different platforms to open stores, which platform should you choose? Now you might ask, why can't you choose all platforms and be multi-channel? The answer is—it depends on the brand. Since Tmall contains more than 50% of the market share and has the majority of the traffic, the book will mostly be concentrating on this platform. However, other brands will be increasingly choosing more and more platforms to suit their consumer tastes. For instance, 得物 Dé wù is a new platform specifically for streetwear. Niche platforms are bound to emerge and take a piece of the pie similar to how there are multiple types of platforms in the US in addition to Amazon.

Payment Apps

It's impossible for ecommerce apps to part from payment. And so, the next two apps make up the majority of what consumers are using today. Contrary to the west in which most transactions are done via credit card, ecommerce transactions in China are largely done via either Alipay or Wechat Pay depending on whether you are shopping on an Alibaba ecommerce platform or a Tencent-backed platform.

Alipay

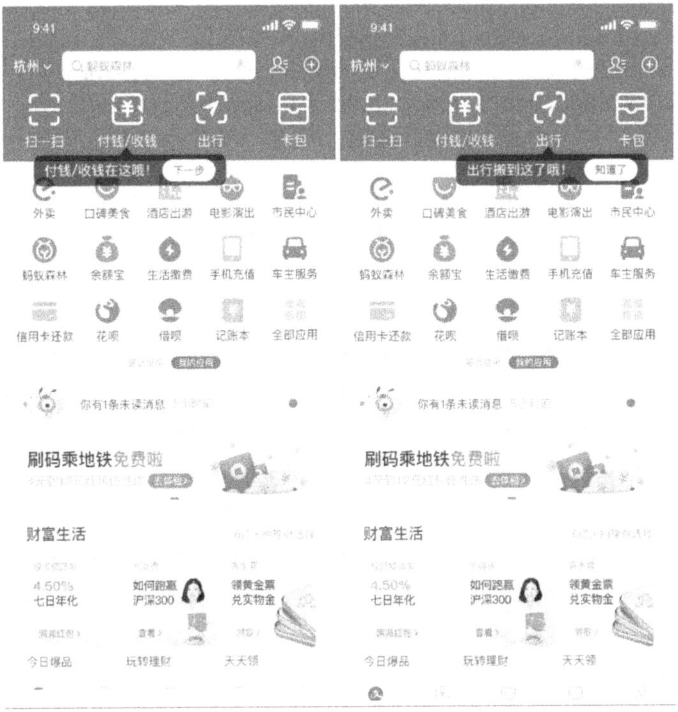

Screenshot of the home page of Alipay

While at Alibaba, I also had the fortune to work in its payment department as a Product Manager in helping overseas Chinese to use their Alipay while outside of China's borders. Alipay is the superapp with its core product in payment. However, one can also hail a taxi, rent a bicycle, invest in stocks in the app as well.

Its origins were first as an escrow payment service to establish trust between buyers and sellers on the Taobao app. The first purported transaction was actually the sale of a camera, listed by a university student. When there was someone interested in purchasing the camera, the seller was met with a problem. *Should the money be sent over first, and then the good shipped or should the seller send the good first and receive the payment later when there were no problems with the product?* Remember, this was the early, early days of the internet, let alone ecommerce! Back then, ecommerce was mostly associated to money laundering and scams. And this was a transaction to be made by two strangers who had never met.

The Taobao team's solution was the creation of Alipay, which would act as a middleman. So the money was given to the platform first, held for safe keeping, as the good made its way to the buyer. After the buyer had received the good and made sure the product was okay, the platform released payment to the seller.

From there on, Alipay evolved from a B2B merchant tool to a B2C consumer tool as Alipay rolled out online payments to consumers. With the advent of the iPhone, it wasn't until 2016 that mobile payments were massively adopted by offline merchant stores. And as more and more stores began accepting this type of personal online wallet, consumers began to adopt this tool in masse.

Today this historic camera is located in Building 9 of the Xixi campus museum as a reminder of the humble beginnings of Taobao.

Alipay and the Coronavirus

I should add here the importance of Alipay as China fought off Coronavirus in its homeland. This might be hard to imagine, but because Alipay worked closely with the government, and because of the ubiquity of the app, most buildings referred to a citizen's Alipay health code. This team was momentous in developing a solution that helped China curb its rate to zero.

The way this works is everyone will have a code displaying a code of either green, yellow or red. Having a green code meant you were able to travel anywhere in the city. A yellow code meant you were restricted in entering into some public buildings such as hospitals and schools. If you had a red code, buildings will be turning you away. Because your location was constantly tracked by the app, if there was a positive case near your GPS location, your code would turn yellow or red since you would also have the chance of being positive. While travelling, provincial border patrol will also be checking your code, and would refuse you if your code was red. By restricting access of those who did not show green codes was how China was able to contain the spread of its cases.

Alipay's Health Code page

WeChat Pay

WeChat Pay is a direct competitor to Alipay's payment product. To date, both wallets claim they are number one in China, however, these numbers are constantly in flux. Similar to Alipay, because Wechat is already a super app, its payment function or wallet function is just another reason for Wechat users to stay and revisit the app during the day. Contrasting to the Alipay and Taobao world, in which both apps are separated, Tencent's messaging app and payment app are together which retains the user for much longer and time spent in app is also much longer than simply Taobao or Alipay.

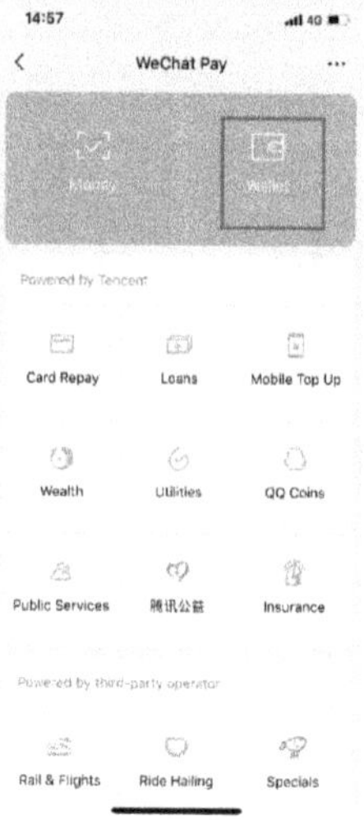

Wechat Pay's Wallet page

Breaking the Walls of the Garden

You've seen that funny Youtube video in your Messenger app, right? Something that your friend sent to you because she thought it was funny. Or that Amazon link in your Telegram because your boyfriend thought it would make a nice gift for the birthday of your roommate coming up? Well in China, all of this used to be hard to do.

Contrary to the west, in which there are no restrictions on which app can talk to each other, the Chinese app environment is one that prioritizes seclusion. Because each app is hosted by a gargantuan technology conglomerate that is seeking to cover all industries in its creation of super apps, each of the large tech companies seek to block its rival, preventing traffic flowing from its own app to another. For instance, if you wanted to share a Taobao link on your Wechat Friend Circle, Wechat will deem the link useless. To combat this, Taobao created a series of code words that the user would need to copy and paste in order to a share a link. Or, if a user wanted to share a Douyin video that he or she found amusing, the user would have to download the entire video to completion, containing the watermark of the video and a searchable ID at the right hand corner of the video and then upload this video to the user's Wechat circle.

Just imagine the amount of time required to do such a thing! So you guessed it, users are disincentivized to do such a thing, and so videos or content from another app is rarely shared on Chinese social media. We can continue down the chain however, because things are blocked both ways. If you had Wechat pay as your only payment app, you will probably not be able to purchase anything on Taobao which will instead welcome you only to Alipay.

Blockage like this is very similar to how the Chinese government had blocked Facebook and Google to grow its own suite of apps further in its home base. When this happened, it allowed the Baidu and Alibaba to grow locally at home. In a similar realm, when super apps are blocking the interchangeability of other apps to be used, they are also growing their own pool of functions. For instance, though Douyin started with allowing Taobao links to be embedded in its video app, they began blocking the function when they wanted to construct their own ecommerce platform. When Taobao merchants could no longer user their regular means of pooling traffic to their Taobao stores, they were able to adapt by simply opening a Douyin store instead.

However, this is all changing. In July 2021, the government vowed to allow the interoperability between super apps in the interest of the user. "Ensuring normal access to legal URLs is the basic requirement for developing the internet," a senior official from China's Ministry of Industry and Information Technology said at the MIIT press conference. Who do you think will be the biggest winner from this decision? Something to think about.

So now that you know the lay of the land, and the many players, next we will dive deep into ecommerce theories and fundamentals.

Works Cited

Achim, A. (2019). The growing influence of little red book. *Jing Daily*. Retrieved from: https://jingdaily.com/the-growing-influence-of-little-red-book/

https://www.alibabagroup.com/en/ir/presentations/Investor_Day_2020_AlibabaDigital.pdf

Ge, M. (2021). Major tech companies in China unbrick walled gardens to integrate rival payment services. *KR Asia*. Retrieved from: https://kr-asia.com/major-tech-companies-in-china-unbrick-walled-gardens-to-integrate-rival-payment-services

Kharpal, A. (2019). Everything you need to know about WeChat—China's billion-user messaging app. *CNBC*. Retrieved from: https://www.cnbc.com/2019/02/04/what-is-wechat-china-biggest-messaging-app.html

Kharpal, A. (2021). *Kuaishou's $5 billion IPO: Everything you need to know about the TikTok rival*. CNBC. Retrieved from: https://www.cnbc.com/2021/02/05/kuaishou-ipo-everything-you-need-to-know-about-the-tiktok-rival.html

Lee, E. (2018). The incredible rise of Pinduoduo, China's newest force in ecommerce. *Techcrunch*. Retrieved from: https://techcrunch.com/2018/07/26/the-incredible-rise-of-pinduoduo/

Liao, R. (2014). Danmu so popular on China's online video sites that it enters the cinema. *Technode*. Retrieved from: https://technode.com/2014/08/07/others-theater-can-see-comments-screen-real-time/

Niewenhuis, L. (2019). The difference between TikTok and Douyin. *SupChina*. Retrieved from: https://supchina.com/2019/09/25/the-difference-between-tiktok-and-douyin/

Stevenson, A. (2021). JD Logistics, the delivery arm of the Chinese e-commerce giant, gains in its I.P.O. *NY Times*. Retrieved from: https://www.nytimes.com/2021/05/28/business/jd-logistics-the-delivery-arm-of-the-chinese-e-commerce-giant-gains-in-its-ipo.html

Tindall, R. (2021). *What is zhihu and how can it help your brand in China?* China Britain Business Council. Retrieved from: https://www.cbbc.org/news-insights/what-zhihu-and-how-can-it-help-your-brand-china

Vaswani, K. (2021). *The race to create the world's next super-app*. Retrieved from: https://www.bbc.com/news/business-55929418

Xinhuanet. (2020). *Alipay's health code landed in more than 100 cities in 7 days, "China speed" for digital epidemic prevention支付宝健康码7天落地超100城 数字化防疫跑出"中国速度"*. Retrieved from: http://www.xinhuanet.com/tech/2020-02/19/c_1125596647.htm

CHAPTER 2

Frameworks and Concepts

The Golden Triangle of Chinese Ecommerce

The next portion of this chapter might get a little technical and theoretical, but it is crucial to learn about the underlying framework that makes this platform tick. Before we deep dive into how to market and what type of consumer to pick, I first need to introduce the full concept of what Tmall is based on.

Behold, the Golden triangle (imagine the below glowing with angelic reprise).

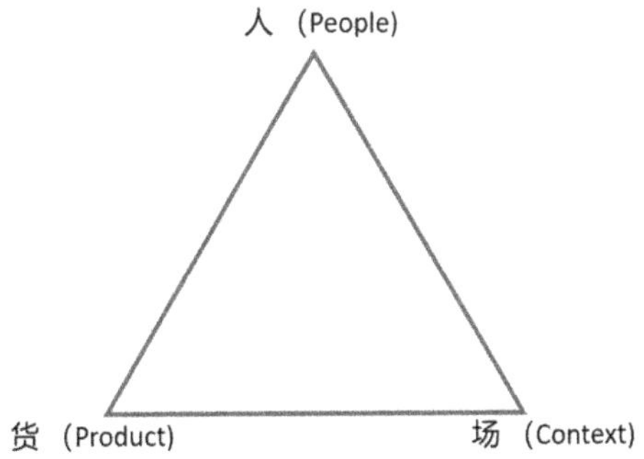

In Chinese, this is commonly known as the foundation of ecommerce: 人货场 rén huò chǎng or otherwise translated, "People, Products,

S. Gai, *Ecommerce Reimagined*,
https://doi.org/10.1007/978-981-19-0003-7_2

Context". Every brand will analyze their store based on this type of framework. Let's deep dive into each corner of this triangle.

People: This is probably the most important aspect of the triangle since it will cause a change to the other two pieces if the People piece changes. Ultimately, it is asking who the consumer is and adjusting everything else about the brand based on who the consumer is. Is the target consumer men or women? What is their age and profession? What tier city does the target consumer live in? These will all factor into the next two pieces which is what exact Product (second corner of the triangle to sell and what Context (third corner of the triangle) to bring it in.

Products: A brand can offer many different types of products. This varies from categories to the specific size of the product, or for instance, the packaging of a product, which includes the marketing message. An eyeshadow palette for instance, that is branded two different ways can cause two different types of price points which will impact revenue greatly. A brand should consider how many SKU's it wishes to bring in and which SKU's. Does it want to focus on one hot-selling product and use this to birth a new brand or does it want to represent a family of products that will craft the brand story?

Context: The third piece to the triangle is perhaps the most confusing to understand, as the Chinese equivalent word is very hard to use a single English word to translate. (Even on Tmall official slide decks, I have seen many variations of the word.) In a nutshell, it is the "space" (physical or virtual) that the product is displayed. This is, once again, dependent on the first two things, who the product is for and what the product is. In physical terms, it is asking "where" the produce is placed, in a physical store, shopping mall, by the counters in a convenience store and so on. Virtually, it is asking *where* inside the app it is placed. (There are hundreds of banner spaces in Taobao for instance) or even which app it can appear, whether a supermarket app, a niche category app or something else.

The combination of these three factors form the foundation of a brand or a brand's flagship store within the app. It will also affect the type of marketing the brand will choose to employ whether in app or out of app. It is crucial for a brand owner to define these main three pillars before proceeding to the next step of crafting the brand's entry strategy.

But first, let's do a deeper dive into People.

Consumer Market—The Eight Consumer Profiles in China Ecommerce

Before we jump into the consumer profiles, I need to preface the explanation of the profiles with China's Tier System. The differences between Tier 1, 2 and 3 cities is mainly in income and GDP per capita. Tier 1 cities are more well off while Tier 4 and up cities are considered more rural. As we move inland geographically in China, we will also see that the topography is to change where larger cities that are coastal have towering skyscrapers while Tier 4 and up cities will likely see flatter farmland.

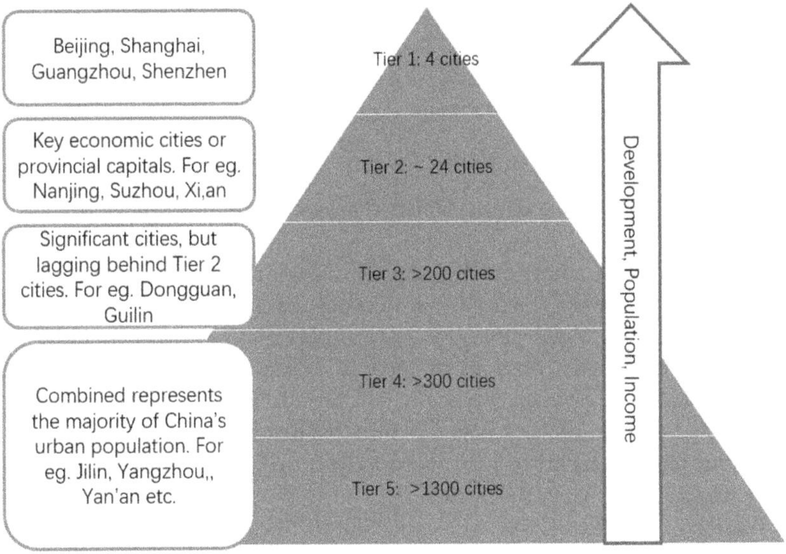

In 2018, Tmall worked with Bain to develop what is now known in the market as the eight consumer profiles in China. Three factors were combined: physical location (which type of city consumers were from), age and consumption power. Physical locations range from the Tier 1–7 cities in China. For instance, Beijing, Shanghai, Shenzhen are considered Tier 1 cities. These are also commonly known cities in China, as well as the largest ones. There are also Tier 2 cities such as Dalian, Chengdu, Changsha. Age has been commonly separated out from young consumers such as those just over 18 years old to senior citizens. Consumption ability is then separated from L1 to L6 in which L1 is the lowest consumption ability and L6 being the highest. Professions are sometimes designated with blue collar and white collar accordingly. If we were to mesh all three together, we would obtain the following breakdown of roles.

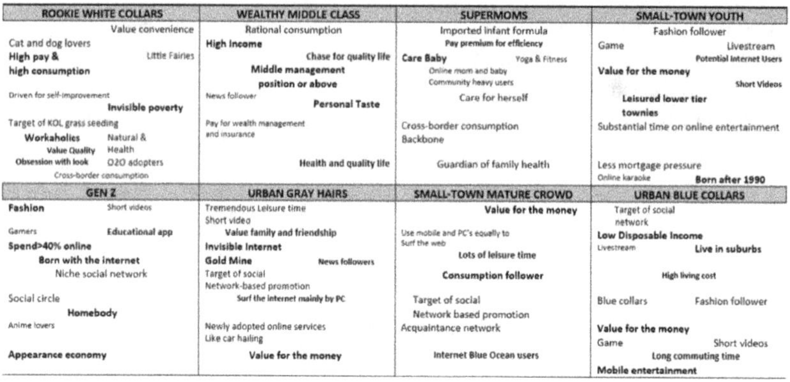

ROOKIE WHITE COLLARS
Value convenience
Cat and dog lovers
High pay & high consumption
Little Fairies
Driven for self-improvement
Invisible poverty
Target of KOL grass seeding
Workaholics
Natural & Health
Value Quality
Obsession with look
O2O adopters
Cross-border consumption
WEALTHY MIDDLE CLASS
Rational consumption
High Income
Chase for quality life
Middle management position or above
News follower
Personal Taste
Pay for wealth management and insurance
Health and quality life
SUPERMOMS
Imported infant formula
Pay premium for efficiency
Care Baby
Yoga & Fitness
Online mom and baby
Community heavy users
Care for herself
Cross-border consumption
Backbone
Guardian of family health
SMALL-TOWN YOUTH
Fashion follower
Game
Livestream
Potential Internet Users
Value for the money
Short Videos
Leisured lower tier townies
Substantial time on online entertainment
Less mortgage pressure
Online karaoke
Born after 1990
GEN Z
Fashion
Short videos
Gamers
Educational app
Spend>40% online
Born with the internet
Niche social network
Social circle
Homebody
Anime lovers
Appearance economy
URBAN GRAY HAIRS
Tremendous Leisure time
Short video
Value family and friendship
Invisible Internet
Gold Mine
News followers
Target of social
Network-based promotion
Surf the internet mainly by PC
Newly adopted online services
Like car hailing
Value for the money
SMALL-TOWN MATURE CROWD
Value for the money
Use mobile and PC's equally to Surf the web
Lots of leisure time
Consumption follower
Target of social
Network based promotion
Acquaintance network
Internet Blue Ocean users
URBAN BLUE COLLARS
Target of social network
Low Disposable Income
Livestream
Live in suburbs
High living cost
Blue collars
Fashion follower
Value for the money
Game
Short videos
Long commuting time
Mobile entertainment

Source: Bain's analysis of Tmall's eight consumer groups

Rookie White Collars are now age 25–35 (or the generation of people born in the 85's or 90's) who live in tier 1–3 cities. Most people are office workers. Their purchase ability is L3 and above. They are not afraid to spend for their needs. Because of their fast pace of life, they are willing to spend money for convenience. This group has an annual spending growth rate of around 20% from 2016 to 2018 according to Bain's report following China's trend of urbanization of more people moving to large cities where there are better jobs.

Wealthy Middle Class are age 35–40, born in 70's and 80's. Mostly civil servants or in corporate middle or senior management; their purchasing power is greater than L3. Their consumption patterns follow close to the type of brands they prefer. They are the group most likely to purchase luxury products. However, their tendency is to shop offline because they grew up in an era of offline shopping, gradually adopting ecommerce throughout the years. They are not prone to emotional buying compared to younger counterparts.

Supermoms are women who are pregnant or have children under the age of 12. They live in Tier 1–3 cities with consumption ability of L3 and above. They love their children, are aware of health effects of products, concerned with chemicals and artificial things as they seek to be educated consumers. They are likely to spend money in fitness and yoga in recent years following burgeoning trends. They are the main shoppers for their families and are willing to pay a premium for convenience. Among all groups, they have the strongest spending power, because of the number of categories and brands they buy, their shopping frequency and the amount they spend.

Gen Z consists of students or others born after 1995 or 2000. They are digital natives. There is a term called 剁手 duò shǒu which means "to cut one's hand off". Though this might seem highly violent, aggressive and bloody, this is part of China's internet language to comically depict certain consumers who can't control their spending habits so much that they should "chop their hands off". They like to try new things. They care about the "look" of a product, big consumers of AGC, and what their friends are using. Unlike their older counterparts, they value trendy items over established brands and are major fans of insurgent brands. This group represented the fastest per-capita spending growth on Tmall and Taobao FMCG.

Small-Town Youth are consumers in their 20s–30s in tier 4 or smaller cities. They follow the trends from their Rookie White collar counterparts and are interested in what this group is buying as this is the profile that they aspire to become. Because of the type of city they live in, they do not have a big mortgage to pay off so will have enough leisure money for spending. They have a lot of free time and will spend an ample amount of time in apps such as Douyin or Kuaishou.

Urban Gray Hairs are consumers age 50 and up. Born before the 70s, they live in tier 1–3 cities. They have substantial wealth because of their sizeable pensions, but still vary on spending because of the context they grew up in China. The major event that made a difference in their lives is the Cultural Revolution. Thus, this group will never spending emotionally or uncontrollably. They are used to shopping offline, and are not adept in participating in online ecommerce. This is the most challenging group to bring online. Some of which do not have WeChat. However, because of the low penetration rate, this group is considered the biggest potential to bring online for some brands.

Small-Town Mature Crowd are consumers older than 35 and live in tier 4 or smaller cities. They appreciate value-for-money products as they do not have exorbitant allowance every month so they are concentrated on basic needs first. With their slow pace of life, they typically have an abundance of time to watch videos or news online. They are more acquainted to shopping offline. The app Pinduoduo has captured a much larger share of this group than Taobao. They registered the lowest per-capita FMCG spending on Tmall and Taobao of any group in 2018.

Urban Blue Collars age 25–45, are less affluent consumers in tier 1–3 cities with consumption ability L2 and below. Because they live in big cities, but do not have the same salary as their White Collar counterparts, they are more interested in getting value-for-money products and will buy fewer items. Their professions are likely to be in transportation, retail or service industries.

Please note that these eight major consumer groups are simply from a model that was developed recently. There very well may be certain groups that are more niche or specific to your brand. Perhaps you are interested in a certain dad population, or hardcore athletes, or pet lovers. Whatever "type of consumer", it is important to fully draw out your ideal type of consumer.

Merchandising

Next up is Product. So you have a brand, and now you have picked your target market, what type of products are you going to use? Many brands, when they enter China, make sure they are selling a different set of products to change the brand impression this brand has back home. For instance, I recently met the Head of Online Sales for Ecco, a Danish shoe brand. I'm sure they are not foreign to many fashionistas. Their price point and brand image in each country has been different. In Europe for instance, they are considered mid or high end. In the US, they are mid low end. In China, though, they are a mid-high end brand. So if you are a faltering brand in your home market, when you are looking towards China, there is definitely a chance for a new birth of the brand. When Hollister and A&F for instance, were faltering in the US and forgotten by the high school generation who had outgrown their clothes, they entered China and captured a decent size of the Chinese market. Pizza Hut, a middle-class brand in the US upholding the hallmark of fast food pizza, rebranded in China to share with its consumers a mid-to-high end dining menu. This is now a location in which young Chinese consumers will go to for dates.

Hero products: this is a set of products that has made the brand successful, or a product that most people think of if the brand name is mentioned. For Apple, it is the iPhone, even though Apple sells numerous SKUs. For SKII, it is their Pitera Essence. Hero products are products that have tested through the times and are usually products with very high repurchase rates. It defines the quality and perception of the brand in consumers' minds, so it is very important to determine which SKU should be deemed the Hero product since much of the advertising spend would be used on this item. When a trend catches on in China, it explodes in numbers that is difficult to fathom for some brands because of the sheer number of consumers in China versus the market size at home. Thus, it is also important to choose a product that has stable and elastic supply chains so that supply can meet the demand if the latter were to suddenly increase.

Hook products: Maybe the hero product is actually quite expensive and a big investment from the consumer. In that case, Hook Products are SKUs that are designed to "hook" a customer to come into the store. Maybe they are a sample size or smaller size than the product you are selling. Maybe they are a collaboration product with another brand. Or maybe they are a limited edition of some sort. Anything that the brand would like to feature in an external ad that will hook a new customer to come into the store is a Hook product. This is not the product that would define the final perception of the brand in the end.

Re purchase product: are there any products that the brand's loyal fan base wants to purchase again and again? Maybe this product can be packaged for bulk or family size with a larger discount. The below is a screenshot of a subscription product, a function that is available to select products. Things such as fresh milk, diapers, pet food, contact lens, fresh flowers are all perfect items to enable this function since they are purchased again and again. For the merchant, it's great to have a customer commit to buying the same product for a six month period. For the consumer, it's great for them to set it and forget it.

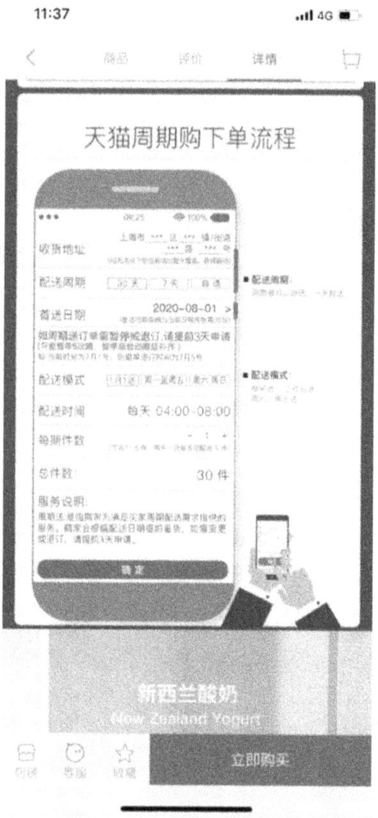

Screenshot of Taobao app on subscription product

Long tail products: These are a set of products are not as favored by the fans of the store, but are also products that cater to a wide variety of fans. This is the set of products that engages with the consumer and allows the consumer to stay in the app for longer. These are products that cater to fringe consumer profiles, perhaps a couple of years older or younger than the main consumer.

Marketing—In vs Out of App

So now that we have introduced People and Products, the next most important piece is the Context, or the set of conditions to make the purchase happen. In a nutshell, it is condensed to Marketing. How do we sell products and grow stores? We further divide marketing out in two large branches: **in app and out of app marketing.**

The difference between in app and out of app marketing is very simple, one is inside the app that you are participating in, the other is all marketing activities done outside of the app, such as another app to drive traffic to yours or anything done in the physical space.

In app marketing within Tmall is quite complicated. One can understand this realm to be mostly dominated by Alimama, the business unit within Alibaba that is most similar to Google Adwords. By investing in Alimama, a brand has a chance to raise the relevance of its product to a consumer, apply SEO on the product or make the product appear to its target audience. Out of app marketing can be presented on Sina Weibo (Chinese Twitter), Little Red Book, Wechat, Bilibili, Kuai, Douyin, Youku (a version of Chinese Netflix). The idea is to drive traffic to your store inside the Taobao or Tmall app. Out of marketing can also be done in a physical space such as a pop up store, an advertisement on TV, a poster in the metro station and so on.

In App Marketing

In app marketing can be further broken down into campaign marketing (platform-led campaigns), marketing IP's, and Alimama as we uncover them one by one.

The First Double 11

"Singles Day" in China, November 11th, or 11/11, is the busiest online shopping day of the year in China. Brands offer huge discounts and can generate up to 50% of their annual revenue. In 2021, Alibaba recorded a gross merchandise value, or GMV of $84 billion USD on Singles Day. But Double 11's were not always large, neither were they even a tradition.

In 2017, I had spoken to the Head of Marketing at Tmall Global, who was the first Project Manager of Double 11. Back then, Tmall wasn't yet a department. It was still called Taobao. In 2009, merchants were simply told to slash their prices by 50%. The below is a poster from the first campaign. Adidas was already one of the anchor brands there along with Jack Jones who saw the highest sales revenue during that period.

Physical print poster ad of the first Double 11 in 2009

Today, discounts are a lot more complicated, so much so that every year, KOLs from Bilibili (Chinese version of Youtube) have shot videos documenting the difficulty of calculating the sale price of an item. It wasn't until a couple of years later where campaigns today is divided into several types of discounts:

1. 购物津贴 gòu wù jīn tiē (Platform-provided coupon)
2. 品类券 pǐn lèi quàn (Platform-provided category coupon)
3. 店铺券 diàn pū quàn (Store-provided coupon for all items in the store)
4. 新人券 xīn rén quàn (Store-provided coupon for new users to the store)

For instance, let's test you as a consumer. This is a screenshot of an item that was in a recent campaign:

The original price for this item is 479. However, it is Double 11 season! Which means there are many types of discounts to use such as store coupons, platform coupons and also a reduction in price if the item was purchased within the first couple of hours of the campaign starting. If there is a special price of 383 in the first hour of the sale, and there is a 10 RMB store coupon, a 300 minus 30 RMB platform coupon, a 200 minus 30 fashion category coupon, what should be the price of the item?

The answer is 313, as listed in bold red in the photo, *only if you purchased in the first hour of the sale.*

Over the years, because of the emergence of many different types of coupons, consumers have also become confused as to what is a discount that is useable, and during what instance. There was a famous viral video made by PapiJiang, a famous KOL in China that made fun of Tmall's complicated algorithm. Shortly thereafter, Tmall began to order all merchants to clearly list out the correct price for their products within the product photo so that consumers can be clearer on the correct price instead of pulling out their calculators every step of the way. However, they did not get rid of category coupons, store coupons or platform coupons. There are now more coupons such as "green" product coupons as well as coupons for first-time buyers.

Campaigns

Today, all campaigns are divided in two categories: S level and A level, where the difference between the two is in the amount of traffic participating stores will receive and how much Tmall will promote outside the app. S level campaigns are Double 11, 618 Mid Year Sale, Chinese New Year's etc., where Tmall will buy physical ad space and invite specific celebrities to endorse the campaign. The most expensive piece of out-of-app advertising occurs during Chinese New Year when all Chinese people, no matter which city you are from, are glued to their screens for the New Year Spring Gala, (this is almost the same as a Super Bowl event, where even in the US, each second of advertisement is worth millions of dollars).

A-level campaigns are more specific to a certain category, and more flexible to change and adjust according to goals of the category.

The below is an outline of all of the major S level campaigns that occur every year.

	Jan	Feb	Mar	Apr	May	Jun	Jul	Aug	Sep	Oct	Nov	Dec
Festival	Spring Festival Valentine's Day		Women's Day	Earth Day	Mother's Day 520	Father's Day		Chinese Valentine's Day			Thanks-giving	Christmas
Tmall Campaign	Spring Festival Valentine's Day		3.8 Women's Day	Mom & Baby	5.5	6.18		8.8 (Members' Day)	9.9 (Flash sale)	10.10	11.11	12.12
Category & Brand Campaign	Super Brand Day; Super Category Day											

Important Festivals to Breakdown:

Spring Festival: Contrary to the western calendar in which New Year's is on Jan 1, Chinese New Year is usually in late Jan or Feb. The special cultural piece to note here is that most Chinese families will purchase gifts to bring home to their parents and families, which causes a spike in traffic and sales of most stores. Even though, this event occurs in Jan, it can also be termed as the End of Year sale, because this is the last sale to happen before factories and brands wrap up a year's work and shut down during the holidays. Some factories will prep to be closed to the entire month, even stretching into the weeks after Chinese New Year.

3.8: March 8 is International Women's Day, but the day is much more significant in China where for some companies, women workers are allowed to take a half day off. Most brands that pertain to women such as cosmetics and fashion will use this event as a boost to their annual sales.

6.18: Also known as the Mid Year Sale, usually lasts from June 1 to June 18, in two different "waves", with sales volumes making a U shape with the highest peaks at the ends. This is usually the second largest sale event, after Double 11.

8.8: Also known as Member's Day. Alibaba has a membership system that ties its users from Tmall to Eleme (food delivery) to Youku (content system). A special discount is provided to its members that other brands can participate in.

9.9: The word of nine has the same sound as alcohol in Chinese, thus the biggest category for this festival is usually wine and food.

11.11: Double 11 has its origins deeply rooted in university life. The most widely accepted story is that the holiday grew out of Nanjing University's dorm culture. While young men have a familial pressure to consider marriage during university, dating and relationships is actually something some men would like to avoid. In 1993, four male students of Nanjing University's dorm discussed how they could break away from familial pressures and instead celebrate their bachelorhood. The date, 11 November (11/11), was chosen because the number1 resembles a bare stick. The idea eventually spread to other universities before Alibaba captured the idea to anchor its first sales events towards young consumers who were indeed single. Today, brands will take their Double 11 numbers as a health check pulse on how well they are doing in comparison to their competitors, as the revenue might be half of the annual sales for some brands, during Double 11.

12.12: A Taobao-led event, rather than a Tmall-led event, 1212 originally started as a Taobao exclusive end of year sale event. Now, the event has floated over to Tmall and has Tmall merchants participate as well.

The below is a screenshot captured from the 9.9 festival in 2021. All product photos that have emerged is recommended to me based on a recommendation algorithm that has taken into consideration my past purchasing behavior, the brands I like, and what the system thinks that I will likely to click on.

Campaign page for 99 campaign

Brands often ask me, do I have to do marketing myself after I join your platform or does the platform take care of this? The real answer is a little bit of both. Some other brands will also very much care if they must follow every single sale the platform is conducting. And the answer to that is it depends. The good thing about following a platform's schedule is naturally, the brand will be advertising for themselves during the campaign, so the merchant does not need to plan out their own marketing events. At the same time, brands might already have their own events such as a summer sale or winter sale. This can be conducted anytime by the brand itself.

After each campaign, Tmall will disclose the ranking of different brands in a certain category. The below is an example taken from the coffee category. The platform then uses these rankings to determine what type of extra resources to provide to these brands in future campaigns. For some brands, this rank board is everything. Some brands like Adidas and Nike will race until the last minute to see who is number one in a certain category. I remember one Double 11, we had two water brands competing for the number one spot, and at the last hour, the CEO would pour more resources into Alimama marketing products, or additional resources to contribute as much as they can in the last couple of minutes in GMV just to beat its direct competitor.

Investors for brands are also very interested in these rankings, as this is a pulse-check on how well a brand is performing and may adjust their investment strategies after results.

618 Campaign results from Tmall Food

This type of brand comparison has also arrived in southeast Asia with Lazada. The below is a snippet of the Fashion category in the recent 99 promotion of Lazada.

Lazada's 99 campaign results for Fashion

The Concept of Horse Racing

Underlying the display of each algorithm is horse racing or in Chinese, 赛马 sài mǎ。Similar to its name that evokes a gambling game, it is when the platform is observing two products or two stores and seeing which one will outrace the other in terms of sales. This observance is highly significant for Chinese platforms versus western ones.

This philosophy even extends into HR and organization structure. Sometimes different things can only be accomplished with select individuals. Putting two different people or BU's on the same project might have different results. One might fail, the other might succeed, so "horse race" was invented to describe an internal business' decision to put two players on a similar path and see which one wins. When you are locked to one team trying to achieve a goal, you are limited to the power and resources of that team. People, time, etc. are all limited. But when you split this goal to two or more separate teams, suddenly you have two ideas on how to tackle one problem, two ways of operations. The best usually wins.

Marketing IP's

There are many notable Marketing IP's that have been built throughout the years that merchants now participate in. One that is of prime importance is called 聚划算 jù huá suàn or the flash sale. Items are discounted for a limited amount of time. This is one of the items on the home page that has a massive amount of traffic. Because of bargain-hunters, the platform enables the shopper to first add to cart, and then for the product to be purchased when the discounted price is in effect.

Screenshot of Taobao app, Flash Sale page

Another IP is called **Hey Box**, mostly used to showcase new products from a brand. Usually these products have no discounts attached as they are the newest series or addition for a brand. There is a special mini program within the app to showcase all Hey Box items of all brands. Fans of a particular brand would pay particular attention to this icon.

Screenshot of Taobao app, Hey Box page

Another IP is the **Super Day** series. The below is a Super Brand Day for Lancôme. The photo on the left is in the Taobao app while the one on the right is a display image in Little Red Book which is out of app. These days are incredibly difficult to book in an app such as Tmall because of the number of brands vying to craft such a day. Usually these days are seen as a mini Double 11 for the brand in which the sales generated from the brand equates to the sales generated during a Double 11.

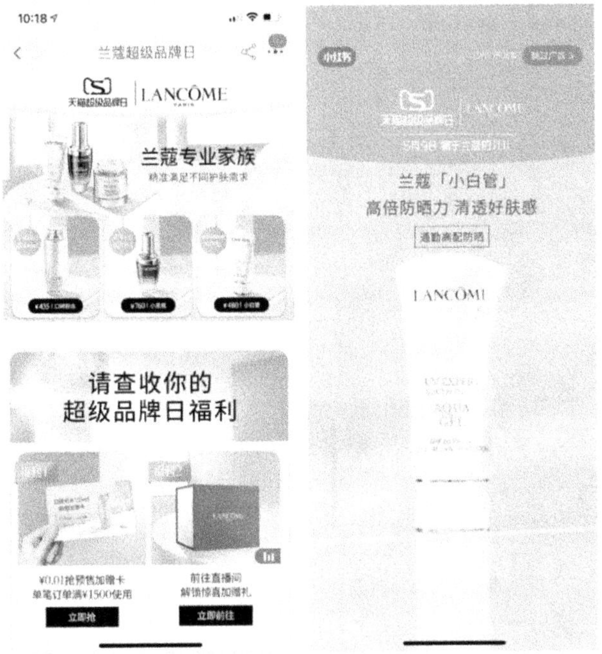

Screenshot of Taobao app, Super Brand Day example

Certain categories are chosen to be displayed in the app to emphasize the popularity of a given category. These are usually categories with high growth rates. These events are called Super Category Days. Some interesting examples have been robot garbage cans, smart mirrors, 5G cell phones and other trends. These are usually started by the category manager who bids for the day internally.

The below is a game IP that is always on during Double 11. From "piling cats" to "city mazes", there is always an element of gaming that is applied to increase traffic. There are mini scavenger hunts and tasks for users to complete. As soon as they complete them, they win points and unlock "hongbaos" or "red packets" that has coupons or money in them to spend during the campaign. Games also get very social as each user pulls in family and friends to join their team to earn more points.

Taobao screenshot of the game played during Double 11

Brand Page

Similar to the KOL pages within Little Red Book, brands can also build pages in their brand hub. This is where most of the content from the brand is displayed. Every time a new product is launched or a new celebrity is featured, the post will show up here and directly reach and engage with fans of the brand.

Taobao screenshot of the Brand Page of Innisfree

Programmatic Marketing—Alimama

Technically, Alimama content can be a whole chapter itself, as it is the very complicated back engine of the entire suite of advertising products on Tmall. This is very similar to Google's set of products in Google Ads. Brands can select a certain group of consumer to target to enable impressions of this brand. For our purposes, I will just highlight four major products as the most common products:

直通车 zhí tōng chē **Direct train** is the ability for brands to spend money on a certain search term. Search terms can be the brand name, a misspelling of the brand name (since some customers may not be able to spell the word correctly), a competitor's brand name, or a category term.

In the below example, champagne is searched, and the first box is the brand that had invested ad dollars in the word champagne.

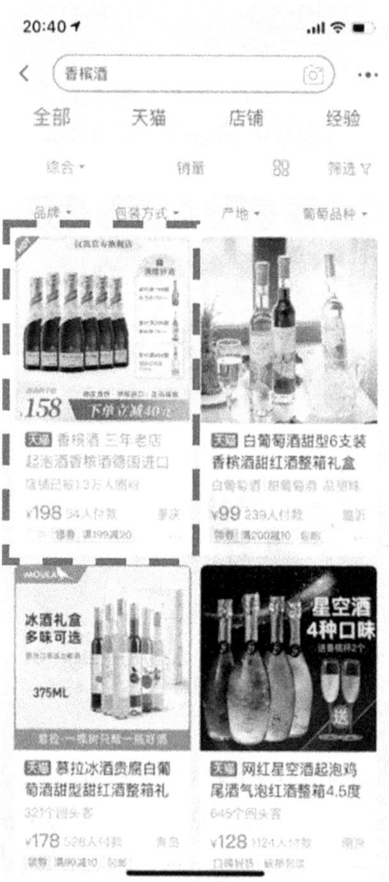

Taobao screenshot of search word champagne

钻展 zuān zhǎn **Diamond display** is another popular product in which brands can target new customers by displaying an ad banner. These banners are queued up according to the relevancy of a certain product. For instance, when the platform knows I am a man, most likely it will not be targeting tampons (unless this was a very heavily searched term.

Husbands can purchase them for their wives!) The below screenshot is one where COS is being targeted to me.

Taobao screenshot of COSís Diamond Display

品销宝 pǐn xiāo bǎo **Star search** directly queues up a store page when a customer searches for the store name. This resource is mostly given to flagship stores where they would like to be displayed higher than a distributor store. For instance, if you were to search Martell, an alcohol brand, all stores carrying Martell will show up. However, because the flagship store is the one that is the most official channel to purchase the product, the brand might want to open this function to direct more traffic to their store.

Taobao screenshot of search word champagne

猜你喜欢 cāi nǐ xǐ huān Finally, brands can also invest money in the **Discovery** section of the app, which is an endless scroll of products in the bottom of the home page. Personally, I've discovered many new brands this way. This endless stream of products is curated for the user, so the user would find this stream of products highly relevant or interesting as potential consumer. By investing money in this product, the brand will have a higher chance of being seen to the consumers the platform deems as relevant to the brand.

Out of App Marketing

The importance of doing out of app marketing is to ensure there is a steady stream of traffic flowing into the store in case the in app marketing reaches a ceiling. It is also easier to create content outside of the app and drive that traffic into the app. This is similar to a brand in the west creating videos on Tik Tok or sharing photos on Instagram that then has a link attached which funnels the user to the brand's ecommerce site. Prior to the emergence of Tik Tok, most brands would embed a link to a Youtube video. These are all termed Out of App marketing. The difference is, the suite of apps in China is absent of Tik Tok, Instagram, and Youtube. Instead, the most common types of platforms to do this are Little Red Book, Bilibili, Weibo, Douyin, Kuaishou and Zhihu, to name a few. Most of these are content platforms with millions of eyeballs, with a user base that rivals that of Taobao.

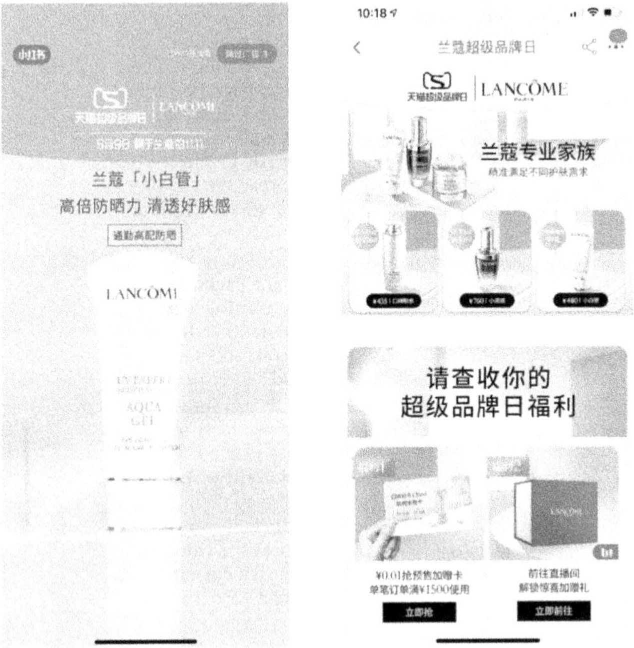

Screenshot of Taobao app, Super Brand Day example

The above is an example of out of app marketing for Lancôme's Super Brand Day. Advertising is done in Little Red Book and prompts users to return to Taobao to search, or, depending in the app, if the user clicks into the ad, they can also be redirected. Returning back to the "walled garden" analogy in Chapter 1, this could happen if the two apps are indeed friendly with each other. However, most of the time, Tmall still wishes to advertise in large traffic apps, but the other large traffic app will not allow brands to directly proceed to the other app after clicking. In these cases, the user needs to go back to Tmall to search themselves.

The below table illustrates the most common out of app marketing channels which we had touched up in Chapter 1 when we introduced them. Some channels are better for reaching certain audiences such as Bilibili, Kuaishou or Little Red Book.

Marketing channel	*App description*	*How advertising is done in this platform*	*Potential impact on traffic*
WeChat	Chat app, similar to Facebook or Whatsapp	1. Brands create a Wechat page that users can follow. The wechat page becomes the app's blog site 2. Brands can also advertise in the discovery section of a user's friend's update page	High
Weibo	Chinese equivalent of Twitter	Brands create an account page that users can follow or employ other KOLs to write about the brand	High
Youku	Chinese equivalent of Youtube	Brands can insert their products into shows that are produced by Youku or display their products in the format of a video ad before videos on the platform are playing	Low

(continued)

(continued)

Marketing channel	*App description*	*How advertising is done in this platform*	*Potential impact on traffic*
Little Red Book	A mash of Instagram and Tik Tok	Popular among young women in the post 95, 90's generation. Brands hire KOLs to create journal entries and short videos in the format of content on this platform	High
Douyin	Mother brand of Tiktok	Brands hire KOLs to livestream their product or create short videos in the format of content on this platform	High
Kuaishou	Similar to Douyin but targeted towards 2nd to 6th tier cities	Popular among higher tiered cities or rural-based cities instead of Tier 1 cities. Brands hire KOLs to livestream their product or create short videos in the format of content on this platform	High
Bilibili	Video sharing app themed around games, comics and animation	Because of the size of the ACG economy in China, brands who are interested in Gen Z or fans of ACG and anime will advertise here in the format of content in a video	Medium
Zhihu	Chinese equivalent of Quora	Brands can create content such as product reviews and brand comparisons on this channel	Low

(continued)

(continued)

Marketing channel	*App description*	*How advertising is done in this platform*	*Potential impact on traffic*
Baidu	Chinese equivalent of Google	Though Google is a highly revered marketing channel in the west, Baidu has less of an importance in China because Chinese consumers will directly search within a shopping app for purchase instead of searching on Baidu first	Low

KOLs and Affiliate Marketing

Finally, 淘客 táo kè is the **Affiliate marketing** program for Taobao. Stores can set an affiliate marketing product and find a KOL to give this link to. For every order the KOL sells, he or she can get a percentage of the revenue of the product. This is a fast way to engage in social commerce and reap the rewards of the fanbase of these KOLs. These product links can be inserted anywhere and will accumulate in earnings for the KOL. When livestreamers first started out, they were given these links to sell during their livestreams.

Seeding and Harvest

"Seeding" or 种草 zhǒng cǎo is a commonly used term in Chinese marketing lingo. It means to sow a seed or plant a seed of interest for a consumer whether that is through an ad, a product review or a short video on Douyin. "Harvest" or 收割 shōu gē or 拔草 bá cǎo is the ideal end result of the earlier word, which in essence means generating a sale of the product.

This phenomenon is now embedded into Tmall data products in the format of AIPL which stands for Awareness, Interest, Purchase and Loyalty. This will be explained more in depth in the next few sections.

Perhaps the best piece of advice that I can give to a brand before they venture into China is to find the right set of KOLs to champion your product. Nowadays, KOLs will need a lot more than simply compensation for a set amount to make a video or commission for every unit sold. The larger the KOL, the more they have to lose if they are recommending a brand that runs contrary to their audience or a brand that they don't' believe in. There are many product tradeshows in which each merchant will advertise specifically to a room full of KOLs. It is then up to them to decide whether to stand behind a product. Some brands go so far as to co-develop their product with the chosen KOL since this is the person who knows his or her audience best in terms of content marketing, packaging and price.

KOC's and KOL's, What's the Difference?

Around 2017, another term emerged, the KOC or otherwise known as the Key Opinion Consumer. The difference between the two is one has many followers and the other has little to no followers. A brand usually will need to employ both sets of partners in order to sell on behalf of its brand. Some brands have also only employed KOC's to sell their brand. Some KOC's also become KOC's inadvertently. Upon reviewing a certain product, their post, because of the algorithm of the platform rushes the review upward and provides enough exposure to the review to be further reviewed by other users. If the brand instantly contacts the KOC, then they will be able to use this person again for a further post.

Some brands prefer to use more KOCs than KOLs because of the authenticity of KOCs. KOLs sometimes are also overly decorated and photo-shopped to reflect real life consumers. Though that can be effective in some occasions, it is simply not realistic while KOC's are more reflective and representative where more consumers can relate to.

Co-marketing with the Platform

Tmall has also introduced 天合计划 tiān hé jì huà for brands to co-market with them. This becomes especially important during campaign season in which Tmall is in a traffic grab with other competing platforms such as JD. Tmall is interested in offline exposure and allows brands to co-brand with them. For instance, the below photo is a photo taken in Hong Kong at a very busy Metro station called Causeway Bay. The blue part can be replaced by any brand thereby showcasing itself but at the same time advertising with Tmall.

Sometimes the brand also wants to have offline exposure whether in airports, bus stations or in front of buildings. Sometimes a brand has a piece of the marketing budget allotted for this channel every year. The brand in this case can choose to co-market with the platform. As long as the red banner is added to the physical ad, the brand can log this into a system and accumulate "points" to spend within the platform such as trading in traffic.

When I project-managed a Super Category Day for my brands in the food sector, the brands would enter into an internal system the placements they had and upload proof of the designs. In turn, the platform provided them with traffic for the Super Category Day. If the brand is willing to share a major KOL or celebrity with the platform to use, the platform will provide extra points.

When my role migrated to Tmall Hong Kong, I designed the platform's first monetization product which was an omnichannel ad product that allowed brands to co-market with us.

Public and Private Spheres of Traffic

A public sphere of traffic is one in which a user discovers a brand while browsing the full platform of Taobao. An increasingly popularized terminology is Private Sphere of Traffic. This concept started taking off circa 2019 when Wechat introduced mini programs. The idea here is that brands are tired of having their traffic shared with other merchants and possible competitors. For instance, Taobao will always recommend "Items that are similar" to the user if they find the user has viewed something but did not purchase. The point of this is for the platform still be able to sell something. Since the platform is incentivized just to make a sale, it doesn't matter which merchant caused this transaction to happen. But if you were the brand and you had just spent money to bring outside traffic in, to then have your precious user convert in you competitors' store, that would be quite a loss of ROI, wouldn't it?

Thus, "Private Sphere" came into play for brands who want to return to the once.com model where the product displayed was only from the brand. This is why Wechat mini programs are burgeoning in creation as more brands want to direct the users they accumulated in Tmall to migrate to Wechat. The mini program will act as an app or singular website for the brand, which means there will be no other competition on that channel inside the brand's mini program. This is what we call a private sphere of traffic and is the ultimate goal of the brand. This functions in a similar format to selling on Amazon. After consumers have discovered and grown trust towards this new brand, the new brand might want to migrate its users to a single website to facilitate repurchase to avoid the cut taken by Amazon.

AIPL

Similar to the Golden Triangle of ecommerce of People, Products and Context, the AIPL model is also part of the foundation of how ecommerce works in China. The main function of the AIPL model is to guide a brand to ultimately convert consumers and have them repurchase. It is divided into four cases:

Awareness: If you are a new brand, how will people know you? The first step for any brand on Tmall is to gain awareness, recognition that you exist.

Interest: This is the next step to convert "Aware" customers to "Interested" customers. The next step is to have potential consumers to take interest in your brand. This is perhaps the slowest and hardest piece to build. Do you have an interesting story? Is your product unique in the market? What element of your brand can actually hold interest? Maybe you will enlist a KOL to evoke interest on your behalf. Maybe a small celebrity might help.

Purchase: This is when the consumer has converted and has purchased your product for the first time.

Loyalty: This is when a first-time buyer has come back and repurchased an item. Maybe they have now joined your membership program or have become ambassadors. Most businesses are built from a group of loyal followers instead of constantly converting new customers.

The below table is an illustration of where to advertise to build up each step.

AIPL	*Alibaba product*	*Description*
Awareness	Diamond Display (Zhizuan)	The platform will show consumers that the platform has deemed suitable for the brand
	HeyBox (Xiaoheihe)	Specifically for new product launches
	Livestream Room	For a brand to communicate directly to consumers
Interest	Recommended Goods (Youhaohuo)	Content channel for brands to write about their top products
	Direct Train (Zhitongche)	SEO of a search term
	Star Store (Pingxiaobao)	Elevate search ranking of store
Purchase	Flash Sale (Juhuasuan)	Sells the product for a cheaper price for a short amount of time
Loyalty	Favorite Brands Portal (Guanzhupinpai)	Similar to Instagram, display content from all brands that a user follows
	Brand Account	Place for brand to share news and product releases
	Loyalty Program	Tmall offers function for brands to offer loyalty benefits to their customers

Breakdown of the Old Ecommerce Equation

The below is a fundamental equation that has been taught in ecommerce schools around the country.

$$\textbf{GMV} = \textbf{traffic} \times \textbf{basket size} \times \textbf{conversion rate}$$

GMV:	This stands for Gross Merchandise Value which also means the total revenue that was sold on the platform.
Traffic:	This is the number of unique visitors that has arrived into the store.
Customer basket size:	This is the amount of GMV that each customer has purchased.
Conversion rate:	This is the percentage of customers that bought something from the store.

By multiplying these numbers together, we get the GMV for a store. When we are setting goals on how much a store should be selling in a year, we would break this number then down to the monthly revenues. For instance, November will be the biggest sales month because most stores have Double 11 as the largest campaign. June has 618 so will also be a big month. The months after these large campaigns, though, will have a steep drop revenue. And this is normal.

Within a monthly revenue goal, all stores should have an estimate of the amount of daily traffic. If traffic numbers are not at the optimal value, the store manager needs to find ways to find additional traffic, whether that's through out of app marketing or in app marketing. Customer basket size can also be increased by suggesting the customer to add to cart items that are complementary to the main product, or products in larger sizes or quantities to give to a friend or stock up on. Conversion rates will normally bounce up or down depending on the discount provided. Conversion rates will rise during campaign season. But this is also a good gauge of your marketing message. Is your message resonating with consumers? What is the average conversion rate of your industry? For instance, fashion brands tend to have historically lower conversion rates, than say, electronics, where products are usually a single common SKU, like the iPhone. People will generally be more certain of their purchase of, say, an iPhone or Airpods than a specific piece of clothing from a clothing brand. Fashion brands will tend to secure a large amount of traffic that will simply "browse" the items without purchase.

Breakdown of the New Equation

Recently the platform has evolved to think about GMV differently and that is to tie it more with the number of users the brand already has, insert the brand more closely to the user, and to consider the user from a longer-term perspective.

$$\textbf{GMV} = \textbf{ARPU} \times \textbf{Users}$$

Users: Converted buyers
ARPU: Average revenue per user

Users can be further broken down by the type of consumer, think back to the eight different types of consumers. Where are the majority number of buyers? Perhaps you have a large set of Gen Z, but you also want to increase the penetration rate of New Mom's as an alternative set of buyers.

ARPU can be further broken down by monthly revenue or annual revenue. This is highly significant for repurchase. It is much easier for an old customer to repurchase than to obtain a new customer. So the point here is how do we get our user to purchase again from us? Is it through a new design, a cross over product, a sale, a new marketing message?

By multiplying these numbers together, we also get the GMV for a store. Why are we migrating to this type of equation? Because at the end of the day, the focus is on the consumer and what type of consumer you can target and penetrate. The old equation focuses too much in singular events while the second equation is much more long-term focused.

Data Analysis

Perhaps the most useful feature of Tmall and its set of products is the data analysis products they have for free to use by the brand. Data products work in a free-mium model in which the basic tier is readily available for small and medium size businesses. For large brands, there are more advanced data products that larger brands will hire a special team or external company to work on called an ISV. Certain TP's will actually have this as a service that they will charge extra. We will go over the different types of TP's in Chapter 4.

生意参谋—*Business Analysis*

生意参谋 shēngyì cānmóu (Business Gauge) is a basic tool that is free of charge for brands to monitor data regarding their store. Showing data such as traffic, conversion rate, average basket size, and ranking against competitors, the Business Gauge product allows store managers to analyze store data to make business decisions for adjustment of the store. The below is a small splash of data points that one can see from the backend.

Traffic

- Total traffic entered
- Traffic that converted
- What type of traffic

Product

- Hero SKU
- Highest conversion SKU
- Lowest conversion SKU

Customer

- Consumer age, gender, income, location
- Highest conversion consumer

Marketing

- Alimama product resulting in highest conversion
- Campaign marketing

Competition

- Which competitors are taking traffic
- Most similar store to your store in Tmall
- Your rank vs. competitors (by conversion rate, traffic level, GMV)

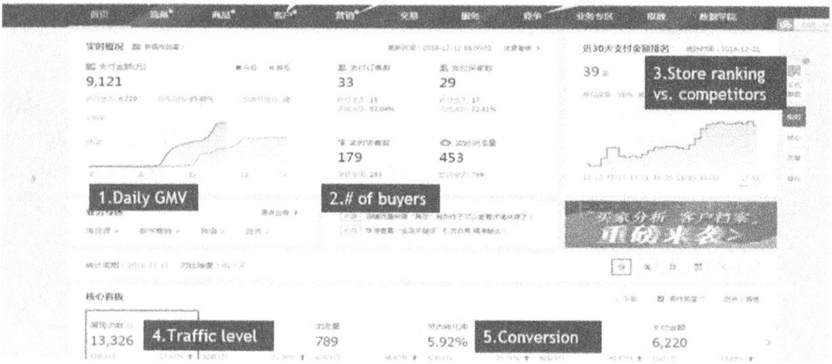

Screenshot of 生意参谋 dashboard

Data Bank

The use of Data Bank is becoming more and more frequent. Brands can combine their own CRM with the data accumulated from Data Bank to provide a more holistic view of a brand's data. The data, it is hypothesized, will be sticky to the platform that brings them the most insights. Many brands trust Tmall to be the primary data partner. As the insights from this piece grows, it becomes harder for the brand to leave. However, the barrier here is that Data Bank is not an easy product to master. There are many ISV's now whose sole job is to do data analysis for a brand, and they can cost up to hundreds of thousands of RMB per analysis.

Uni ID

The big difference between the internet landscape of the west and the BAT world of China is how tied together the data systems are between the apps. Do you remember our breakdown of all of Alibaba in Chapter 1 with all of the different apps spanning across many industries? Ecommerce, offline commerce, payment, short video, travel, and maps are all industries that Alibaba is in. If they can map a single user's behavior across all of these different apps, they will have built a powerful database on these users. Because one user needs a single cell phone number to register and use the app, Alibaba as a whole is able to know its users very well. This ultimately provides brands a highly accurate data product with immensely precise profiles of the consumers they are wanting to target and convert.

In a way, Alibaba is both Google and Amazon combined. Its unique data product and ability to track its users sets the company in a unique position in the face of the other gargantuan tech companies in China. Through its investments and acquisitions throughout the years, it has been able to build a portfolio of companies that can rival its equivalent competitors in the west. The only trick now is whether the Chinese government will allow such data monopolies to grow any larger in the future.

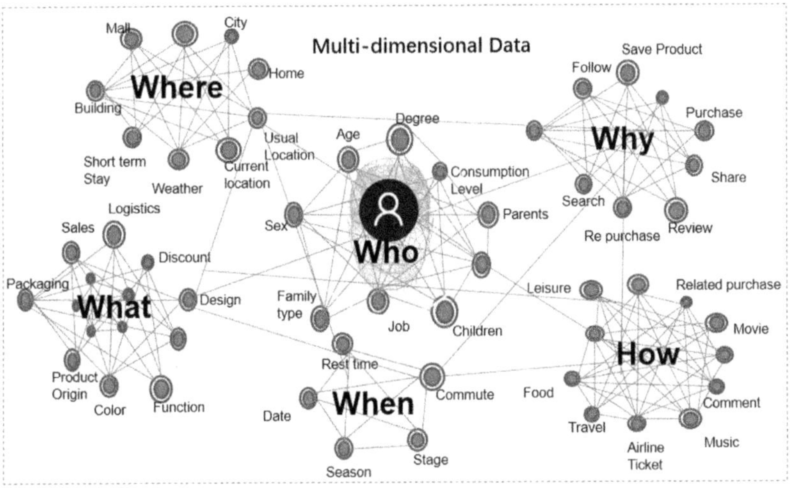

Works Cited

Alimama. (2003a). *什么是直通车 What is direct train?* https://subway.simba.taobao.com/indexnew.jsp#!/home/index?curValue=nav_1_sub_1

Alimama. (2003b). *什么是钻展 What is diamond display?* https://zuanshi.taobao.com/?spm=a2320.7388781.ca214tr8.d9bda87b6.6f372030m12DV9

Alizila. (2017). *Alibaba's new 'Uni marketing' a game changer for brands.* https://www.alizila.com/alibabas-new-uni-marketing-game-changer-brands/

Ding, J., Lannes, B., & Deng, D. (2019). *2019 Online strategic consumer groups report: Innovate for consumers with insights from Big Data.* Bain & Company. https://www.bain.com/insights/2019-online-strategic-consumer-groups-report-innovate-for-consumers-with-insights-from-big-data/#

Luo, J. (2021). To KOL or not to KOL in China. *Jing Daily*. https://jingdaily.com/kols-influencer-strategy-china/

Sina Finance. (2021). *Penetrating the "people, products, context" of retail: not a business model but a technical reconstruction穿透零售的"人货场": 不是商业模式 而是技术重构*. https://finance.sina.com.cn/chanjing/cyxw/2021-01-15/doc-ikftssan6632963.shtml?cre=tianyi&mod=pchp&loc=26&r=0&rfunc=53&tj=cxvertical_pc_hp&tr=12

Wong, D. (2019). *China's city-tier classification: How does it work?* https://www.china-briefing.com/news/chinas-city-tier-classification-defined/

CHAPTER 3

Emerging Trends

The Trend of Livestreaming

Since 2019, livestreaming has been one of the most important ways for a store to engage its followers to make a sale in China. But livestreaming was not always for selling items. The concept of livestreaming is actually nothing new. Back in the day, it was mostly in the format of connecting with strangers on the internet. A host would sing or play guitar, interact with his or her fanbase and receive red packets or 打赏 dá shǎng from the viewers. It wasn't until 2019, that Taobao livestream saw the inevitable way that products had to change to become more appealing to audiences.

Over the years, the way products are displayed has evolved. We progressed from simply listing the product (think Craigslist), to displaying basic photos, to more beautified photos and contextual photos, to short video, to user-generated videos of the product being used in an actual space to livestreaming. The evolution has strived to have the product become closer and closer to the consumer because that's the only way online selling can rival that of an offline store experience.

The first time that I had ever livestreamed was actually in 2017, when I was accompanying a Chinese rap star, Jackson Wang, to LA to attend the American Music Awards. We planted some products throughout the livestream session so that our celebrity can interact with them but that was it, nothing like the direct selling shows that are now dominating the mobile screens of Taobao. Back then, livestreaming had not developed

S. Gai, *Ecommerce Reimagined*,
https://doi.org/10.1007/978-981-19-0003-7_3

into the live selling phenomenon it is today. In 2017, it was mostly a show, used as entertainment, for brand building. The year 2019 was the year during which livestreaming took off to become a common way for stores to sell products online in China.

What Is Livestreaming?

Livestreaming is a concept of selling or sharing products with customers who are joining remotely to watch, chat, and buy.

What Does a Livestream Room Look Like?

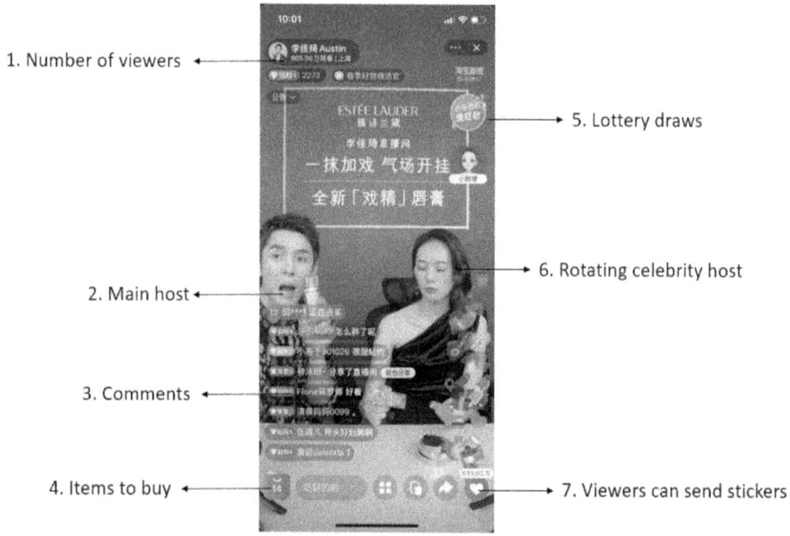

Screenshot of a livestream room with Austin Li

Breakdown of a livestream room:

1. The **number of viewers** is up top. Take note however, that this number is the total number of viewers who have watched and not the current number of people in the room right now. This was a

psychological mechanism that the Taobao product team placed here since viewers will only want to stay in rooms that have very large numbers, instead of being in a room that has only one other viewer. So even if you see a very large number here, there might actually be just one other viewer in the room with you. You will never know.
2. The **main host** will tend to sit on the left side, since from a viewer's perspective, our eyeballs will usually glance from the left to the right when reading across a screen. The main hosts' body will also be directly above the links to the products to guide the viewer to more easily click through the links.
3. **Comments** will fly in throughout the course of the livestream session, typed up and sent in real time, usually with questions about the product or usage of the product.
4. **Items to buy** are placed in a general pool or large shopping cart. After the host has talked about a product, she will place them into the general pool for viewers to buy. Viewers can then flip through the total number of products and at any time click into products that have already been talked about.
5. **Mechanism for engagement** when the viewers are idle: to maintain engagement, the host may instigate a lottery draw to draw for a certain item for free, gamifying the experience.
6. The right placement is usually for a **guest appearance**, either by the host's "helper" or a celebrity which will increase the traffic level of the livestream room.
7. **Likes**: viewers can click on driving up the number of "hearts" or "likes" which will also algorithmically raise the engagement reading of the room to rank the room higher in the main livestream tab.

There are some clear differences that make **livestreaming the ultimate way to sell** things:

1. Live: Livestreams are very intimate, where a live person is talking directly into the camera in a just-in-time fashion for the consumer. Usually, this is someone charismatic, funny or interesting to watch paired with a product, which elevates the liveliness of a product. In ecommerce, product display has evolved from a still photo, to reviews, to a recorded video. It is only natural that a *live* video provides a more immersive experience for the consumer.

2. Interactive: At any time, a consumer can write a question or post a comment which is displayed in real-time to all watchers and the host. The host can then choose to address the comment live and answer the question in front of all viewers. This is a new element of connection that appears between a viewer and the host as both parties interact with the product more deeply.
3. Curation: Popular livestreamers will constantly have hundreds of thousands merchants approach them to sell their products, so their teams will have tested many products in the same category to know truly which product is superior. Thus, in a livestream session, the products are curated towards quality. The livestreamer is the one responsible for customer service after-purchase so if he/she chose a bad product with quality issues, he/she would apologetically be the one to deal with that consequence.
4. Price: What will push a consumer to buy something in a livestream session versus any other time of day? A flash sale will guarantee that the price is lowered for a small period of time so that the consumer feels a greater need to buy the product immediately. Prices for certain products are cheapest in their livestream room, when that product is on promotion. This makes livestreamers extremely powerful as price-sensitive consumers will gradually all flock to her livestream room, which burgeons her number of followers even more.

History of Livestreaming

The act of livestreaming itself is actually an ancient art form since the QVC channel had been around since 1986 in the west! But why was this phenomenon short-lived? The innovation that China had inadvertently made towards livestreaming is creating a seamless user experience for the shopper to buy without the hassle of calling a phone and entering a credit card, and they targeted a much younger consumer target instead of QVC which was targeted towards middle age to senior citizens.

West: The West had begun with QVC as a top shopping channel with viewers tuning in similar to how current viewers were tuning into livestream shows. The next big push into livestreaming in the west was largely made by Twitch, which started with streaming gamers that attracted a unique pool of users. Periscope, began in 2014, mostly to document movements and attracted a social science set of users before it was later acquired by Twitter. Facebook Live began its live footprint in 2015 before also turning on the feature for Instagram. Youtube Live began in 2017 for Youtubers to maintain a closer connection with its fans. And finally Linkedin Live began its live events in time for Covid as the world shut down its advent of in person networking conferences.

China: things started a bit differently. Many small apps started and died that is now difficult to find documentation. A notable survivor that is still quite strong in the livestreaming space is YiZhibo. Originally starting off as social network that connected hosts to other idle users, hosts would receive comments and stickers that the viewers would buy in exchange for the host to hum a tune, sing a song, tell a joke or simply entertain the audience. Momo, originally a dating app, similar to the Tinder of the west began its livestreaming footprint in 2015. Taobao Live began in 2017 also without the structured way of selling it has today. It wasn't until the first anchor hosts came to Taobao and had minor success selling products that Douyin and Kuaishou followed suit.

People have wondered what it is about livestreaming that has grown explosively in China. If we refer back to the Golden Triangle of People Product and Place, we will notice that there is a difference between the interaction of People and Product. A natural progression for ecommerce is to connect the product closer to the consumer. While it started originally as a product listing, it later evolved to photos, then reviews of the product in word format, videos of products, photo reviews, video reviews. The logical next step is for the product to be showcased in real time directly to the customer if there is still a screen between the seller and the customer via livestream. Now the big question is, what can come after livestreaming?

In the last Double 11 campaign, three livestreamers appeared above all others in terms of the amount of products they were able to sell: Viya, Austin Li and Cherie. Their sales combined to a total of 1 billion dollars in sales during Double 11, which is more than many large brands on the platform.

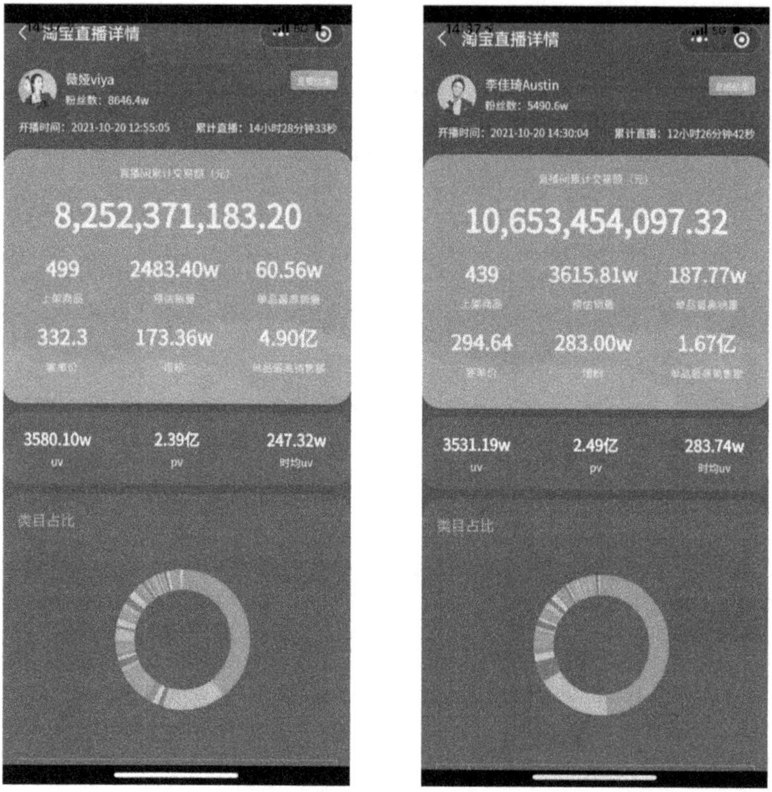

Taobao Livestream dashboard screens of Viya and Austin during Double 11 2021

The cost of having one of these KOLs mention a product for the brand (price as of Mar 2021) is around 40,000 RMB with a 10% commission.

Eg. A product that is priced at 100 RMB and sold for 10,000 in quantity, the brand will have to pay 140,000 RMB for a two minute mention of their product during a livestream session:

$$40,000 + (100 \times 10,000 \times 0.1) = 140,000 \text{ RMB } (\sim 14{,}285 \text{ USD})$$

A KOL would usually be featuring around 80 products a night, so by multiplying those two numbers together, these KOLs are roughly earning $1 million USD a night for talking for four straight hours, the average length of a livestream show. Because hundreds of thousands of merchants send their products to these KOLs, it is quite competitive to obtain a deal. Sometimes, the brands might choose to sell at a loss or earn no profit just to have exposure on the product. Local and global products have launched new products directly in these livestream rooms where each view can be recorded. Brands have discovered this has a much better return on investment than spending large amounts of money on billboards in high-traffic areas without a digital footprint of who has passed by the sign or follow-up as to if the person had bought the product or not.

Why Is the Rise of KOL's Important?

Because the nature of ecommerce is very agile, the rise of KOLs poses a significant threat to the platforms. Whereas before, the platform held most of the power in deciding which products can go on sale or which products will get more traffic than another, with the advent of KOLs and livestreaming and the burgeoning success of these top three livestreamers, the ecommerce space sees a shift in power of price control. If a product is not discounted enough, they might not be chosen to get a spot in a livestream show, thus removing the possibility of traffic for the product. Thus, the KOLs start controlling more and more power of a product from its price, to marketing message, or to packaging. Because the feedback for each product comes through in a live format, brands will also use KOLs and livestream rooms as dependable market research. KOLs then become a unified service for research and sales for brands. If a KOL can amass enough brands and customers through ongoing sessions, it is very likely KOLs can leave a platform and start their own platforms if they desire.

Evolution of Livestreaming

There are now 3 major livestreaming platforms: Douyin, Kuaishou and Taobao Live, in increasing order of volume of transactions on each platform. People have often asked me why it is so hard for western markets to replicate this success. And the reason goes back to the ability of the platform to coordinate forces to join together to make a trend happen.

When Taobao Live was created, it set out three major goals. First, to create 100,000 播主 bō zhǔ or KOL's with monthly revenue of more than 10,000 RMB. Second, to create 100 MCN organizations with annual sales of more than 100 million RMB. Third, to release resource packages worth more than 50 billion RMB in total. The last point is the main reason why livestreaming was able to take off. I mean, how does any trend take off in the real world? Tik Tok? Ice Bucket challenge? Hashtagging? Scale is needed. And what is needed for scale to accumulate is an incentive for the users so that user base can grow. So the employees of Tmall began first with incentives for merchants to start livestreaming, and the way they did this was by providing "extra" resources. Things such as an extra red button that flashes on campaign pages or a permanent channel dedicated to livestreaming or increased traffic for merchants who were livestreaming are all ways that the platform incentivized merchants to start livestreaming. When a certain mass was achieved, the merchants who were not partaking in this activity realized that much of the GMV transacted today was on the livestreaming platform, which prompted them to begin livestreaming as well.

Now, about 90% of merchants are livestreaming on a weekly basis, including large brands such as Estee Lauder, Huawei, Lancome, Haier, Xiaomi, Loreal, Shiseido, La mer. The top categories for livestreaming are jewelry, beauty and fashion. Jewelry, for instance, is a prime category for livestreaming since it is usually priced rather high, and would not usually be a good product for ecommerce, but instead offline purchases. However, because of livestreaming, jewelry brands are able to tell the story behind a certain type of stone, and display the product with much more depth than a still photo would in ecommerce.

The current viewership profile for livestreaming is 75% female, born in the 90's, mainly in second and sixth tier cities. Livestreaming actually used to be something that people in the first tier cities would look down on. I've heard many friends back in the day ask themselves why in the world would someone have the spare time to watch someone else talk endlessly about a product instead of simply making the decision to purchase something on their own. A couple of years later, that same exact group of people began to watch livestreams themselves.

Top categories in livestream rooms Taobao Livestream Report 2020

Other categories that have seen a significant rise for livestreaming are cars, furniture, wine, musical instruments, gaming, DIY PC, pets, collectibles, pianos to name a few. Most of these are categories oriented towards a male segment, and this group is definitely on the rise to also develop a habit to watch livestreams.

Today, livestreaming has evolved into something more than just selling. It has become an entertainment source and stress reliever, an ASMR if you will. Similar to someone tuning into a radio station regularly because of the soothing voice of a host, viewers will tune into a livestream room regularly to also listen and watch their favorite hosts. Because of the optimal price points generated by hosts, I personally, for instance, would regularly check back on certain channels simply to see if there was anything to snatch up. I have also found myself to try more and more new brands that I would regularly not be discovering or trying. It has become a point where offline and online ads are working less and less for me to successfully have me convert as a user. Instead, if my favorite livestream host were to tell me about a new brand or product, I have much higher chances of making the purchase.

Livestreaming has also evolved to involve AI robots being the livestream host. While human laborers would need food and sleep, causing a break during a livestream session, robots do not need such things and would be able to continue a livestream session continuously if fed enough content.

Even offline stores has begun the act of livestreaming. Pet stores has one of the highest duration of viewership. Viewers purport that they are soothed when looking at cute puppies run around. Travel livestreaming became very popular during Covid when it is no longer convenient for Chinese tourists to travel abroad. Fliggy, Alibaba's travel department partnered with the Louvre museum and facilitated a livestream tour of the Louvre. Finally, rural livestreaming or traceability livestream became popularized as transparency amongst consumers rose as a need. Farms, for instance, were livestreamed to show which orchard an apple was picked, or which cow was milked to make specific dairy products.

Screenshot of a livestream room with an AI livestreamer

Livestreaming During Covid

Perhaps another reason for the acceleration of adoption of livestreaming was during Covid. While on lockdown, consumers at home still wanted a way to shop and buy groceries. Livestreaming enabled them to experience a way to see and feel the product without physically being there. Even when malls began opening up, consumers were afraid to venture back outside. However, because brick and mortar stores had set up livestream rooms within the floors of the retail space, it was able to not only utilize idle inventory, but also bring personality into an otherwise lifeless store. Intime is a mall owned by Alibaba and it was one of the first brick and mortar stores that enabled its 5000 retail associates to open livestream sessions with each counter. Experiencing a lower than usual traffic, the associates were idle. Thus, some were asked to livestream and others were asked to pack orders. Because the channel for livestream for Intime was directly tied to the Tmall store of Intime, each order that was sold online took inventory from a specific offline location.

Dora Viya

Today Viya, or as she names herself Dora Viya (named after Doraemon, the Japanese cartoon) is the largest livestreamer in China in 2021. She named herself after Doraemon to imitate her ability to share anything and everything in one's home, from the floor tiles to clothing to food. (Doraemon was a cat that had a limitless pouch from which he would pull magical objects) Before she made it in the livestream world however, her humble beginnings began with selling clothes in Guangzhou. She and her husband sold everything they had to continue their clothing business until they were forced to shut down.

Today, she livestreams all types of product categories and promises the best price, creating a new marketing tool within the Taobao ecosystem. She has a team of 200 people handpicking each and every product within every product category. Because of her popularity and ability to bring trust to new brands, many merchants will send free samples to her team. The team then organizes each product according to product category by brand and begin product tests. Some include QA tests, taste tests, usability tests, and develop a thorough and rounded review for each product.

Viya herself will then pick the mostly highly reviewed product and use it herself as verification. Thus, when she is presenting a certain brand for a specific product category, she has already used the product herself and is not blindly selling something because the merchant has compensated her more financially. The credibility of livestreamers rests firmly on the trust of their viewers. If a product demo were to go wrong, her viewers are sure to screen capture and propagate the news to other fans which will later catastrophically spiral into a negative PR event that hurts her brand. This is usually called "翻车" or "the car has toppled over".

Another unique element to her livestream room is her infamous countdown of "5, 4, 3, 2…1" During an actual show, Viya will upload each product link one by one, instead of all at once. In one night, she might be uploading a total of 200 hundred products. The surprise and mystery of what is to come is her way to invite viewers to come back into her room if they've found the room to be quite dull or if they've found her to be talking about a product that is irrelevant to them. Countdowns are present to signal to the consumer to buy. Because the inventory of each product is kept at a certain amount, products can easily sell out if consumers are "too slow" to buy. Her countdown not only adds adrenaline to the exprience but it forces consumers to act without thinking and buy instantly.

Now, Viya is close to running a similar system to a "talk show". She begins at 8 pm during Golden Hour or the hour that has the highest traffic for the app. This is usually a time in China were employees are off work and families have finished dinner, a perfect idle time for consumerism. Because of her consistency in show time and schedule, consumers will also check her room daily to see if there's anything to "pick up". As said earlier, probably the most exigent demand from her team is the price to sell the product at. They will likely require the item to be at Double 11 price (usually the best price of the year) or the lowest price of the year.

Austin Li

Originally someone who was selling lipsticks at a make-up counter on the first floor of a department store, Austin Li had selling skills that was primed for his role as a livestreamer in front of thousands of fans. Comfortable with selling lipstick to women as a man which is already a rarity in China, Austin has a flamboyant voice that drew the attention of many women. Originally specifically zoning into cosmetics, Austin had a niche and loyal fan base. With the frequency of new products uploaded in beauty, Austin had plenty to talk about during his "shows". However, similar to how all KOLs will begin with a niche category, they will later expand to other categories when their audience is wide enough. After all, a woman might pick up a lipstick one day, but will not need a new one everyday. To stay relevant to his customers on a daily basis, he expanded to other categories such as grocery items and home goods to increase purchases.

Celebrities

To add to the festivity of the room, Viya will invite celebrity guests throughout the year to increase traffic and attract new followers. Many celebrities have, by now, tried livestreaming, if not having adopted it permanently. Those who still haven't tried are in large demand to be put into a livestream room to see the effects and ability (good or bad) of the celebrity.

Livestreaming in the Future

Viya and Austin are just two examples of successful livestreamers on the platform. Their fame, though strong, will not be forever. However, the contribution they have made is the way they are working with brands. Because the platform has encouraged brands to directly livestream in their rooms, I predict that the eventual scene of livestreaming will be a very fragmented one, with viewers sticking to the type of KOL they like to watch.

New Retail

In 2016, Jack Ma coined a new term that united online and offline retail. Broken down, it is the synchronization between offline and online resources. Specifically, in products, membership, marketing and service.

Perhaps the most common scenario for New Retail is in fashion since that is an industry that has truly been redefined by a new digital strategy. Take for instance, Uniqlo. Uniqlo will allow its Tmall consumers to shop in the app prior to arriving in a physical store, and arrive at the store to pick up. Because sizes and shapes in Uniqlo are quite standard, shoppers are usually repeat shoppers who have a good idea of their size. They will pre-order the item, an associate will wrap up their order, and the consumer can directly pick up without trying the clothing. This is highly convenient for a time-strapped shopper who does not have the time to run through the entire store only to pick up a simple item. Pick up in store has not been replicated fully to other brands but is estimated to be basic service for future brick and mortar stores.

In Hotwind for example, a fast fashion shoe store, the unique service is omnichannel returns. Because the hardest thing about shoe-selling online is fit, it is very common for the consumer to have chosen a wrong size and need a trade in. Instead of asking the consumer to completely return the old online order and then wait for a new online order to arrive, it is more convenient to open the service for consumers to take their ill-fitting pair of shoes to the store to directly trade in for a new pair at the right size in store.

The following table divides many omnichannel functions for four main pillars: product, service, membership and marketing, the "resources" to be synchronized.

Resource	Function
Product	Scan and review
	Scan and save for later
	Cloud inventory
	Delivery by store
Service	Returns
	In store pick up
	Subscription
Membership	Membership card
	Rewards
	Personalized member interaction
Marketing	Membership benefits
	Coupons

Let's look at each pillar in depth.

Product: when we look at product, we are blurring the designation of "offline" SKUs versus "online" SKUs. Instead, a brand will have shared SKUs and simply a way of knowing which channel a product was sold. Prior to synchronizing Product, a separate pile of inventory would be separated for online channels and another pile for offline channels.

Service: by service, we mean the same type of service one can receive either interacting with the brand online or offline. For instance, if during an offline store, we are able to receive a very personalized service because the sales associate knows the customer by first name, can we also replicate something similar online also? Perhaps going one step further in displaying or recommending products that is personalized to this shopper.

Membership: we have all had membership programs that we have signed up for and not used. Some paid, some unpaid, usually a membership program for a brand is separated from its online and offline arm. Over the years, programs have been synchronized for a brand's dot com and physical store, but is it also possible to synchronize another channel such as the brand's flagship store in a platform? How can we provide the same type of service to the member both online and offline? These are the questions that we consider when we are synchronizing the membership program for a brand.

Marketing: Finally, marketing can also be integrated in terms of discounts and coupons. For instance, why are some coupons only useable online, and some offline? Would we be able to unite the two channel and have them interoperable? If I received an online coupon in my email, I might want to check out the product in person in the physical store. This is when the pillar of Marketing as a resources needs to be synchronized.

The Battle of Online and Offline

Shanghai 2004

"Why would we ever open a Tmall store?" said the Head of China of H&M. "We already have physical stores and if online, we can always build our own online system!"

"It's interoperable. You will see!" Magnus said.

This is a classic battle within a brand team. The group in charge of the physical stores will always be picking a battle with the online team, thinking that one channel will cannibalize the other. But little do they know the benefits of having a footprint online, especially in a traffic-filled platform like Tmall. This is why we have had various traditionally offline retailers and restaurants open up shop on Tmall. Chayan is a highly popular bubble tea store in Changsha, Hunan in China. Queues for the store usually reaches an hour long. Because demand is higher than supply, the brand leaves its consumers wanting a lot more than they can get while travelling in Changsha. The opening of the Tmall online store allows a geographically restricted brand to have a national presence. Though the fresh tea is not sold online, the brand's packaged tea packets and other merchandise is just as popular. Recently in Double 11 2021 Pre Sale days, Chayan achieved top 3 in the teas category.

A big portion of Viya's selling now has evolved from products to experiences such as selling dining certificates or coupons. All major offline-heavy restaurants have all opened, or have considered opening their Tmall store. Some people might find it strange. What is a restaurant doing on an ecommerce platform? From a consumer's perspective, what if you want to continue the great experience you've had with the restaurant at home? Is the physical location hard to reach? If the restaurant is able to open itself to a larger audience like a national ecommerce platform, it becomes 24/7 operable and viewable by its fans.

Hema: The Ultimate Supermarket

Workers in baby blue t-shirts running to and fro through the store, one picking up a couple of carrots, another cradling a watermelon. They are the pick-and-packers, their main job, unboxing and shelving new crates of vegetables, but in their spare time, fulfilling orders that come from the online site. A large aquarium sit in the middle of the estate, housing multicolored fish, restless shrimp, and crawling lobsters that had just arrived from Boston after a cryogenic ride across the Atlantic. Moms wheel shopping carts around the pre-made food area, sipping the last bit of soup from a Xiaolongbao bun, a new brand that had just launched and done well in Tmall. They had seen the brand before, advertised online, and now after having a taste of it in a supermarket, some decided to pack some in their carts.

This is Hema, the supermarket that emphasizes freshness represented by a blue hippo with an oversized mouth, among Alibaba's zoo of animals.

Hema Supermarket is the most well-known form of new retail within Alibaba. A brick and mortar store that began organically within Alibaba, Hema had its important other half of its business as an easy to use online app that was launched at the same time. Unlike other supermarkets in which the brick and mortar would be around for years before its online version was created (always with limited functions at that) users of Hema saw the online app as the remote control of the offline version, with most of the stores' flexibilities, special services viewable directly within the app.

Perhaps the most prominent feature was its 30 minute delivery promise. If it took more than 30 minutes to deliver something, the order would be deemed free of charge. This promise led to the explosive reception from consumers and was the first supermarket to establish the now accepted idea of quick commerce. Hema's delivery fleet was able to achieve deliveries at such speeds because of the proximity of the store to the consumer. The unfortunate end of the stick was that if you lived not within an approximately a 3 km radius, you wouldn't be able to even buy from Hema. One would think this would cause a drop in customers and room for competition to take over. It actually resulted in more loyal users vowing to buy or rent homes closer to Hema locations. The placement of Hema stores caused a surge to surrounding real estate prices and became one of the features of "convenience" for inhabitants in new neighborhoods.

及时配送 Jí Shí Pèi Sòng Just in Time Commerce or Quick Commerce

Since the establishment of Hema's model, merchants in China have experimented with multiple other ideas in terms of fast delivery. Can every store achieve 30 minute delivery? That will depend on the ubiquity of store locations. But can every store in a given surface area at least achieve same day delivery? Possibly! It very much depends on how products are then organized. A couple of years ago, Taobao added a new permanent icon to its home page (there's a pattern here: the businesses that have lasted or aka the experiments that work have ended up in the format of a permanent icon on the home page). The "Instant Delivery" icon represented a group of products that were able to sustain one hour delivery. Consumers will mostly find food and grocery products, but other categories such as Mom and Baby items slowly began joining the ranks. By carving out a specific icon, the app has raised the norm of delivery time for certain merchants, similar to livestreaming and omnichannel, will later become a basic service for online consumers in China.

Quick Commerce

Remember those days when the whole family would hop into their SUV and drive down to the local supermarket, and buy enough food to feed a small village? Those days are gradually disappearing.

Recently there is a new buzzword by the name of Quick Commerce. The idea is that since most young consumers live in concrete jungle cities where their apartments are limited in size, they prefer to not stock up on a certain item, but to get it just-in-time instead.

With the rise of urbanization, the number of small or single-person households is rapidly growing. This has led to a rising demand for delivery of products in small quantities rather than purchasing many items in large quantities at a cheaper price (which is how traditional commerce and e-commerce works).

Quick commerce companies swap traditional brick and mortar warehouses far outside the city center with centrally located cloud stores. This geographical advantage allows them to reach more customers faster, with less friction, and deliver goods from their favorite local stores.

The below graphic illustrates the migration of each step towards quick commerce as it becomes more suitable for the current make up of a family in modern times.

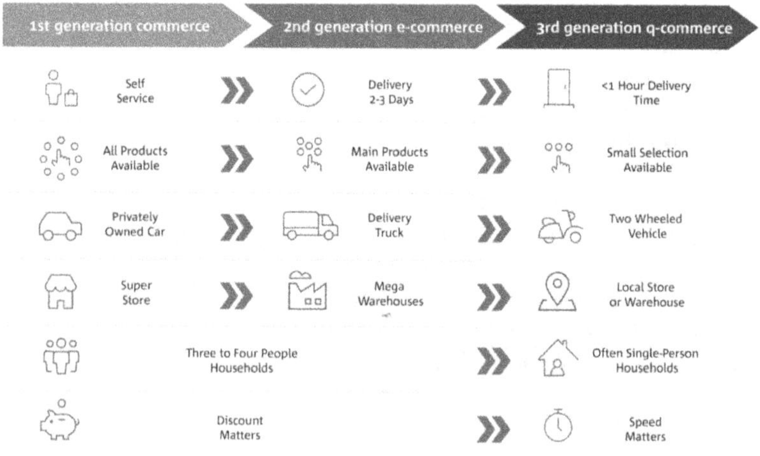

Source: https://www.deliveryhero.com/blog/quick-commerce/

The most amazing experience I had with Quick Commerce was with Luckin Coffee. Yep, that infamous brand that was under a huge PR scandal because they had muddled their numbers, but their brand and product still stands in China with a consistent purchase rate. After about 10 minutes of my order submission on their Wechat mini program, a 蜂鸟 fēng niǎo deliveryman arrived at my door with my coffee, all for 12 rmb (which is around 1.8 USD). Sometimes, I do feel both guilty and spoiled that I can enjoy a service that is as fast and as cheap as this, but at least the delivery man can earn some extra RMB? Most ride electric bikes so at least the environment does not take a hit!

One book that I thoroughly enjoyed that took Quick Commerce to another level is called QualityLand by Marc-Uwe Kling. The book posits that in the future, the clicking of buttons is no longer necessary as the platform will have stored so much data on us, that drone delivery bots would just drops things into our laps haphazardly, because they would be able to accurately predict what is that we wanted to buy before we even need to actively go through the steps of purchase.

Global players such as Foodpanda, Deliveroo have also begun a similar business expansion, into groceries. Through an interview I had with someone in the logistics team of Foodpanda, I understood that the logic for this type of companies to break into ecommerce was perfect, since they were already delivering food items. The easy next step would be for them to increase the number of categories they would cover.

Sheconomy

The Chinese market has nearly 400 million female consumers between the ages of 20 and 60, and their annual consumption expenditures are as high as RMB 10 trillion, which is close to the combined retail markets of Germany, France, and the United Kingdom in Europe. This number is enough to constitute the third largest in the world consumer market.

Increasing levels of education, coupled with a high labor force participation rate, has helped build a foundation for greater financial autonomy. Delayed marriage and a fast-declining birth rate also mean that the consumption habits of female consumers are undergoing significant changes. Gender equality has become a growing topic of discussion online. With more women becoming aware and outspoken about their rights, brands are facing the consequences of creating content deemed sexist or partnering with figures seen as controversial. Simultaneously, demand for content satisfying the needs of female communities has shot up.

The Shenzhen company, PurCotton, was one that I had visited a number of times during my time at Tmall. In 2021, they published an ad that sparked outrage on the internet. A young girl walking alone at night, realizes she has a packet of PurCotton make up removing wipes in her bag, takes it out and starts wiping off her makeup. As a masked man puts his hand on her shoulder, she turns around and smiles at him with a makeup-less face and scares him away. A few days later when the brand began to openly apologize on the internet, netizens had another issue with its apology letter, purporting that there was only one sentence of apology in the letter, followed by one more page of awards and achievements the company had. All in all, this company probably needs a new PR team.

Here, I must also highlight the growth of this consumer segment in its significance from a societal standpoint. As women in the country gradually become more educated and high income earners, they are less and less dependent on their male counterparts. By 2016, women started outnumbering men in higher education programs, accounting for 52.5% of college students and 50.6% of postgraduate students. From 1990 to 2016, the average age for first marriages rose from 22 to 25 for Chinese women, and from 24 to 27 for Chinese men, according to the Chinese Academy of Social Sciences. The figures in big cities are even higher. For example, in Shanghai in 2015, the average age for first marriages was 30 for men and 28 for women. With less money needed to spend on children, they have more money to spend on themselves. From all facets of life from food, travel, fitness, classes to experiences.

Thus, several industries in personal care, cosmetics, travel have seen a significant rise due to this added spending power. These industries has taken topics such as Sheconomy and employed them in their ad campaigns. In 2016 when SKII published a commercial on Leftover women, it had won a Cannes Lion Film award. Leftover women is a colloquial term in China that means women who are above 30 and less eligible to be married. The ad documented the stories of a few women who faced pressure to get married, interviewing herself and her parents of how helpless they were that they weren't able to see their daughter married yet.

Viewers watch a painful struggle and clash of values in two generations that many women in China empathized with. The end of the ad shows an understanding that is finally reached between the parents and the young woman, with the parents succumbing to the daughter's wishes, and respecting her choices.

SK-II's global president Markus Strobel told Bloomberg Businessweek that the campaign "helped the skincare brand increase sales in China by more than 50 percent in nine months. 'This campaign has put us on the map in China and generated extremely positive sentiment among consumers and retailers, helping us win with young professional and executive women.'"

As someone who grew up in China, I was also told by my parents to be 文静 wén jìng, an ideal adjective to describe young girls (this literally translates to "know how to read and be quiet". A silent woman in China had been heralded to be someone ideal to marry. To be outspoken and opinionated was not rewarded as a trait. As I migrated to Canadian classrooms and American universities, my once muted tendencies slowly began to change as I interacted with more perspectives. With the rise of the sheconomy in China, I'm sure many more brands will take advantage in harping on the topic of feminism that we've seen in the west.

The #metoo movement didn't bubble up in China as it had done in west. Instead, it was actually banned in internet searches. Shielded with the words 米兔 mǐ tù (the sound from these two Chinese words sound similar to MeToo), the movement has still been a quiet one. But as more and more sexual harassment cases has been documented in China, more and more women have been more outspoken in their experiences and looking to each other for support and understanding. My prediction is that brands that face these taboo topics head on will have an immediate reception from the female market.

Appealing to Gen Z

The Gen Z consumer market, born between 1996 and 2010 accounts for 17% of China's population but 25% of total expenditure on new brands. Though the Baby Boomer group is actually larger in size and hold most of the consumption power, Gen Z is the most common group targeted by consumer brands.

Why, then, would these brands spend so much marketing dollars to attract this group?

Because this is the future "Boomer" generation. Think about the FMCG brands you grew up with, if you Google their parent companies, most likely they will fall under the family of P&G or Unilever by today. And you will continue to trust these brands. It will take a lot longer for you to buy into a new brand because you have already established loyalty to the mass brands of today. You're already used to buying them. But the younger generation are less "brainwashed" and a lot more receptive to seeing a new brand and then purchasing.

This group has been widely studied in the past couple of months due to some unique combination of characteristics compared to other consumer groups.

1. **Wealth:** This group grew up with less financial restraint than their parents, which contrasts that of a spender born in the 80's or even 90's, who were taught to be frugal and save. Gen Z grew up during a time in China that was experiencing rapid growth and without the shadow the Cultural Revolution their grandparents endured. There is a term called "the moonlight clan" in reference to their constant spending until their monthly salary is depleted. Borrowing money to satisfy consumption needs is common in this group, something that is the opposite in the Boomer generation.
2. **Technology:** this group learned how to use the iPhone and iPad before learning how to drive. They are much more acquainted and comfortable with software and apps. Growing up in an information age, they are more attuned to searching for information instead of being restricted with the information that is taught in traditional schools or from TV. They are digitally-savvy and are adept in checking multiple information sources before making a purchase decision.
3. **Value-based:** They are attracted to the values that stand behind a brand. When money is no longer an issue, this group knows how to "vote" with their dollars (or RMB in this case)! They are disengaged with the mainstream methods of marketing and how products are traditionally brought towards them. Instead, they care about experiences, wanting their horizons to be expanded and seeking to learn new information.

There is an internet meme that describes how different generations in China face the prospect of a tough boss. If a boss tells an employee, you will be fired, the guy born in the 80s will work harder to prove the boss wrong. If a boss reprimands someone born in the 90s, they will talk back to the boss. Tell the Gen Z they need to work harder, they will say, "It's okay, I wanted to leave anyway. I'm firing you instead!"

Though this is commonly known as a joke, it is reflective of the current generation's attitude toward work. This group of people grew up during a time in China that was remiss of poverty or a lack of resources, so labor for them was something elective. Their innate attitude is also reflected in their choices of brands and products. Dissimilar to old counterparts, Gen Z is interested in what is meaningful to them instead of what is meaningful as dictated by their old siblings or parents. This is perhaps why the collectible culture and ACG is so prevalent in China.

ACG, also known as Anime, Comics and Games is a fast-growing trend in China. When I first went to China, I didn't see it as much, but in the years of 2020, I would see, more and more, young people walking around in traditional Chinese clothing. Even at work, at the Alibaba campus, because we have little restrictions on what should be worn while at work, some colleagues would come in, dressed in their favorite ancient Chinese costumes. 汉服 hàn fú is a type of costume from ancient China and also the theme from many different games.

The Gen Z group is especially attracted to this role-playing culture as it plays into their imagination and takes them to a different world where they can assume any character they want. While bars and clubs still dominate the night life activities of people in the west, there has been a new phenomenon developing in China in which young kids are opting to play 沉淀 chén diàn room escape games. These type of games are ones in which a group of people need to dress up and role play a character to then solve a mystery or a murder. A mash of Sleep No More, theater and room escape, these type of games are highly reflective of the imaginative and creative activities that dominate the lives of a young Chinese person.

Recently there are two terms that have been popularized among Gen Z. They are 内卷 nèi juàn (involution) and 躺平 tǎng píng (lying down), the latter being primarily popular among Gen Z. These are two societal phenomenon that illustrate the attitudes of the current generation. The equivalent of Involution in western popular culture is basically the "rat race", an ending cycle of who can work harder to outrace the others. The 996 working culture of "9 am to 9 pm, 6 days a week" was a popular way to describe general Chinese working culture, which formed the Involution pillar. If someone was working overtime by one hour, you'd better work overtime twice as much, otherwise you will be outcompeted by your colleague.

The "lying down" group, or many Gen Z's, in this case, is saying, we know full well the rat race situation, do not want to be part of it, and so we give up, or lie down, in this case. Another term called 佛系 fó xì or to be more "Buddhist" is of a similar camp. To be calm under pressure or to approach things with a more Buddhist mindset will trump those who work harder under pressure.

Of course, the attitudes of Gen Z is not something that is one-size-fits-all. I'm sure there is an adequate amount of Gen Z-er's who have similar characteristics to their older counterparts, but the uniqueness of these traits are very interesting to study from a brand perspective as it changes the narrative for many brands as they target this group.

Made in China

For about a good two decades, after China enacted the great economic opening of its economic and welcomed international trade, Chinese consumers had a love of global brands. Back then, I always felt it comical when Nike, having had factories originally in China, make their product in China, slap on an American label and would be able to sell the product back to Chinese consumers with an international price. Chinese consumers were more than happy to pay the premium. As a young immigrant child shopping in the malls of Canada, I would pick up items of clothing with my mom. "Made in China" for $30? She would ask me to put it back down. "We can find something equivalent in China for half that price, honey," she would say.

The words "made in China" used to categorize things that were cheap or poorly made. However starting in 2018, things took a different turn. We can attribute this turn possibly due to the trade war, Trump's term in office or growing international hostility, but the Chinese consumer is gradually paying more and more attention to local brands, with a young demographic especially interested in supporting locally-grown brands.

Locally termed as 国潮 guó cháo, or in other words, "national and trending", the Chinese love for domestic brands has gotten stronger. Consumers used to prefer to buy foreign brands because it was thought that foreign brands had better quality and better materials. Since so much of marketing is making a consumer feel a certain way when they are using your product, it used to "feel" more international when you were using a foreign product.

One event recently to note is the advent of H&M and its PR statement.

Overnight, a Weibo post spread rapidly across China, at first in fashion circles, and later across all major media outlets. It was the PR department from H&M openly protesting the usage of cotton from Xinjiang. Personally, as someone who is conscious of what both sides were trying to do, I very much understand and empathize that something catastrophic like this can happen. However, in this case, the global PR team of one company does need to remember to double check things with a local PR team before blasting news out from the company to the world.

Or we can look at Dolce & Gabbana, where a new ad had a Chinese girl look at a confused plate of spaghetti with her chopsticks. While the creators of the ad meant the commercial to be something playful, Chinese consumers found the ad to be distasteful and racist. This eventually led to the shutdown of several offline locations and the disappearance of the D&G Tmall store to disappear online. The leadership team had to formally apologize to Chinese consumers. To date, they have not recovered.

I was once asked by a reporter what I thought about the values that celebrities would need to give up if they were to sell to China. Back then I had said that they were making a choice when doing business in China, just like how other organizations were doing business in China. It does not mean that they had to void the values and belief they uphold as a unit but instead to take heed of the culture in China and be more conscious of what to portray when facing Chinese consumers.

In the west, we have all heard of the term "being woke" by now. Even some Americans tell me they can't openly express their feelings without being attacked by Team Woke. Many of my friends, many who are ethnic minorities, say it is like walking on eggshells. China is similar in this sense. All subcultures have sensitive topics that is sore to talk about. Few understand this part about China.

China is an ambiguous market. If you have ever learned about the different ways of global communication, whether direct or indirect, China is definitely of the latter, where one word has layers and layers of meanings and will change according to context. In any type of mass marketing campaign, it is just always best to send it to someone locally to double check on the appropriateness of the content.

Cross Branding

Cross branding, crossover products, or 跨界 kuà jiè is when two brands come together for a collaboration product. Crossover products are not something unique to the Chinese product world. The difference in China is it is taken to extremes where two very different brands or products will collide to create a crossover collaboration.

Most often, these products are created to renew a consumer's interest in a brand or acts as a hook for clicks. Sometimes, the brand completely knows that the product will not be pushing much in inventory, but will definitely serve as an interesting product launch to attract attention.

Here are a few of the interesting cross over products that I've seen (and sometimes eaten!).

1. Baijiu flavored popsicles (Baijiu is a 50% alcohol product)
2. Duck neck flavored cookies (duck neck is a popular snack in China!)
3. Ink flavored soda
4. Beer flavored chips
5. Crawfish mooncakes
6. Stinky tofu ice cream

And these are just a handful. Tasty or not, they definitely catch attention, and this is perhaps the most coveted thing for brands and marketers.

Sometimes, a fast way for a new brand to become relevant locally, cross branding is an interesting way to enter the market. When one brand does not yet have a footing in the type of brand it is representing in the foreign market, it can leverage an established brand locally to help with brand positioning.

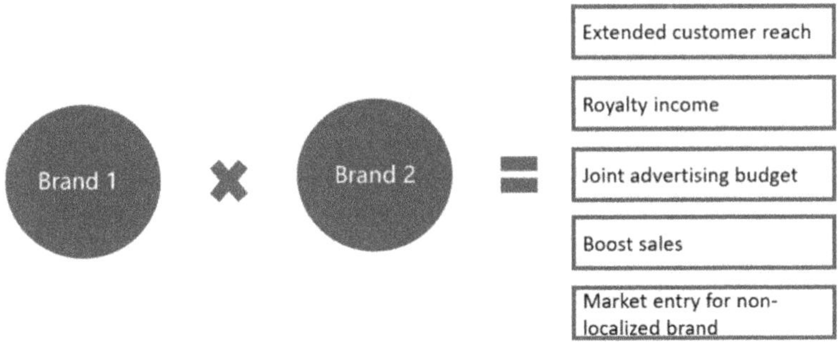

When two disparate brands come together, it creates a symbiotic affect

The below are all IP's that Alifish owns today (partnerships are always expiring and renewing so this list is not up to date) but you get the picture. Alifish is an internal department at Alibaba that buys and owns IP's for brands to rent.

IP's that Alifish has worked with

Usually when a new movie comes out or when a new comic series is released, Alifish will negotiate to include this IP in their platform. This IP is then made available to the 300,000 brands in the ecosystem to use. Brands pay a retainer to Alifish as a deposit and then will pay a commission per item sold. This is a great way for brands to use cool and hip IP's in their products and just change the design, instead of investing in R&D for a whole new set of products.

For instance, Uniqlo has very simple basics. To increase repurchase rates and have their fans come back to their stores, they will collaborate with popular IP's such as Kaws to re-invigorate their brand's relevance.

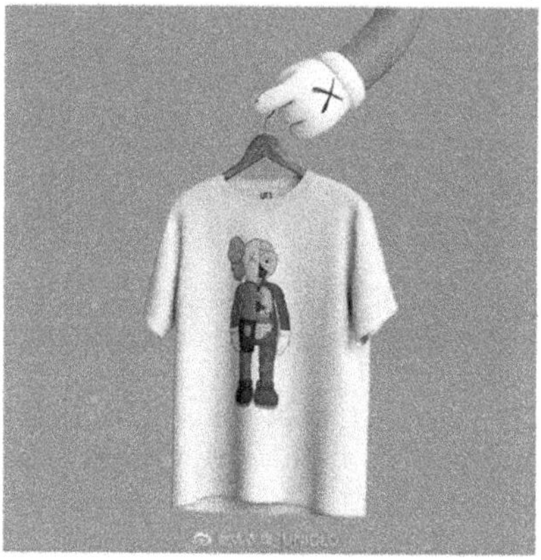

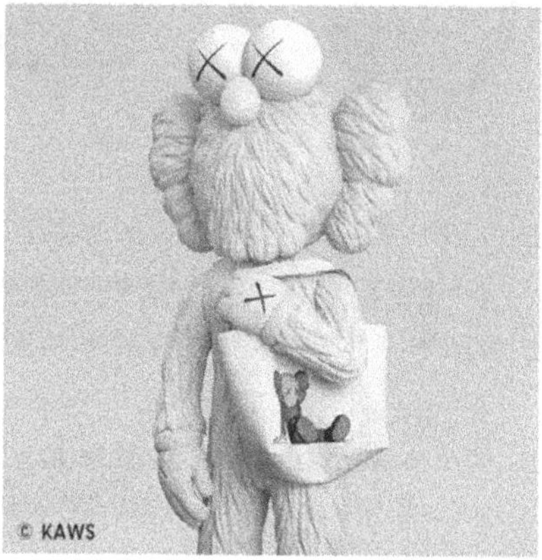

What is also very common are brand and brand collaborations. It's always a sight to see what the design teams from the two brands can come up with.

When two brands come together, there is usually some sort of benefit for both parties otherwise they wouldn't agree to meet in the middle. Either one party is being paid a royalty fee or the other party is benefitting from the traffic that arises from the collaboration.

I was personally part of a collaboration project when a very old milk brand in China wanted to reach younger consumers. The milk brand is called Bright Dairy, a brand that I consumed as a kid.

This is a type of brand that has never changed their logo or look for decades. In Chinese we call this 老字号 lǎo zì hao, or a brand that is very ancient and traditional. The consumers of these brands do grow up and grow out of favor with a brand they had interacted with when they were younger. To become up to date with current trends, it's common for these brands to collaborate with a brand that is already in tune with the current market. We selected from a variety of fashion brands and looked at pricing offered from various brands and ended with INXX.

Through this collaboration, Bright Dairy was also able to elevate its brand image by partnering with a brand that was a lot higher end.

The milk carton was changed into the shape of a cross body bag, and the nutritional facts of milk was turned into the back of a Tshirt. The resulted product sold out in seconds and was later resold on a Craiglist site equivalent for many more times its sale price.

光明
鲜牛奶
INXXSTREET
光明
鲜牛奶

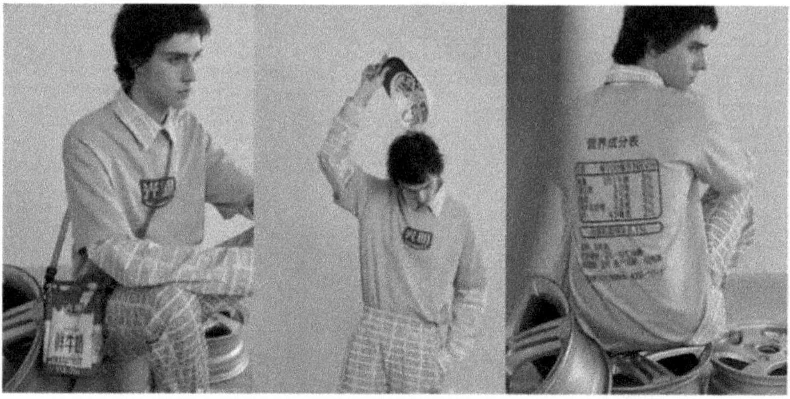

A local sports brand had done something with a famous local newspaper.

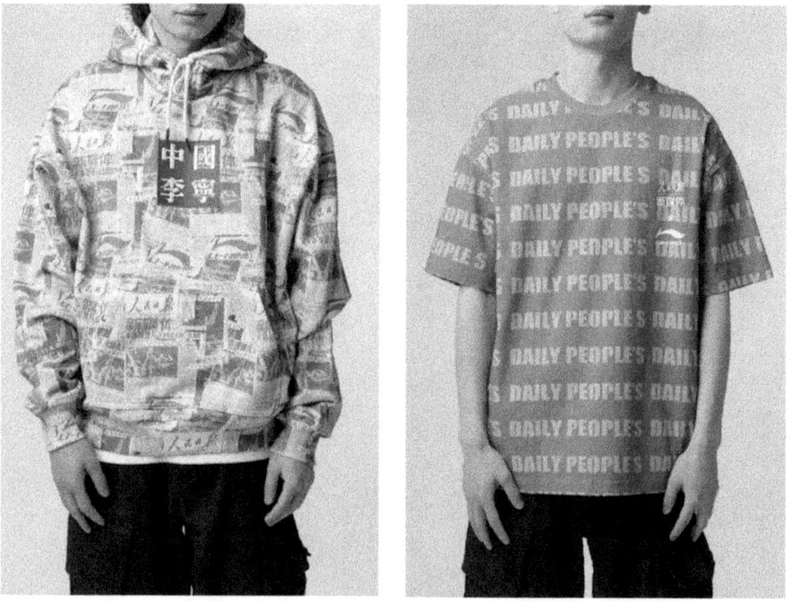

Brand collaboration between Lining and a local Newspaper

International brands such as Coca cola has also done collaborations with local sportswear brands.

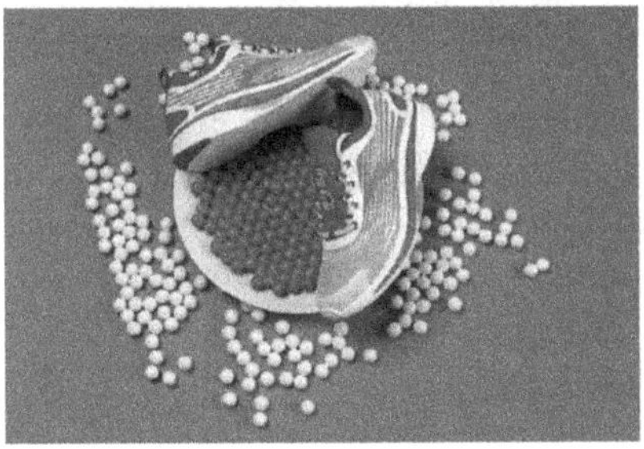
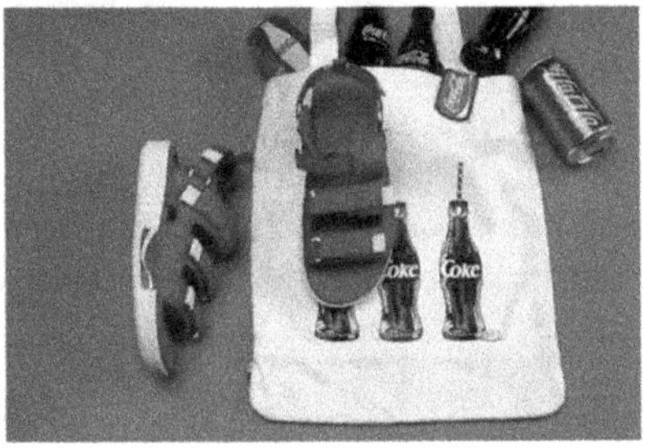

I have also witnessed some very cool and unlikely collaborations throughout the years, one of which is the fashion brand Alexander Wang, a very New Yorker type of fashion brand collaborating with McDonalds.

Collaborations like these pique interest. They're fresh and eye-catching. If paired correctly, they will usually sell out very quickly and generate a lot of buzz for the brand. Some collaboration projects that were meant to be one-time actually might last throughout the ages.

C2M

C2M has recently been more and more popularized as a trend. Also known as **"Customer to Manufacturer"**, it is when customer is dictating what should be made in a factory rather than factories producing products to then test with a consumer market. C2M allows the consumer to directly liaise with the factory in manufacturing something they want. Another way to understand the concept is to crowdsource a given idea or product. Kickstarter is something that has seen success in the West in gathering money before a product is made. Alibaba took this a step further and created a new department called 犀牛 xī niú to liaise with clothing factories to produce products that they knew consumers were interested in. The first brand to emerge is called 暴走的萝莉 bào zǒu de luó lì or "The Girl who Keeps on Walking". An athleisure brand mainly aimed at young consumers, it was made with data from Tmall's insights on the millions of searches performed on a day to day basis, piggy-backing on the rise of athleisure during Covid.

Tmall Innovation Center (TMIC) is a department within Tmall that serves as a market research firm for brands to work with on product innovation. Because Tmall has captured thousands of data points, brands can leverage data from the Data Bank and use TMIC has a set of consultants to look at what searches are trending to provide more insight on what a new product should be. This sort of mechanism is especially interesting for brands because of its unique ability to create a full loop from production creation to sale to feedback.

Fabrice Megarbane, president of L'Oreal North Asia and CEO of L'Oreal China, talked to Alizila's Christine Chou about how partnering with Tmall Innovation Center has helped it develop new products for the Chinese market—in as fast as 59 days. In an interview with Alizila, he purported that usually L'oreal will take months to do testing. In a large CPG company, launching a new product can take 15 or 18 months, but by collaborating with Tmall's data engine, market research can be shortened and the platform allows you as a brand to test a number of iterations of the product before sending it to production.

AI and Avatars

While AI still remains a hotly-debated topic in the west about whether robots will eventually kill us all, in China, AI is rarely seen as something negative. People seem to accept that they will eventually be replaced by robots and they are fine with it. Most people figure there will be another job invented for them.

Since then, Bilibili (the Youtube-like platform introduced in Chapter 1) has experimented with virtual avatars primarily in games. The most prominent brand to experiment with avatars in a consumer-facing perspective is Florasis 华西子 huá xī zǐ, a D2C cosmetics brand that emphasizes on eastern beauty and elements of traditional Chinese culture, something that has been forgotten by the larger global brands that emphasize on western beauty.

For a long time, the "Chinese style" was not so much favored. In a cosmetics industry where large French conglomerates dominate, Florasis shows their products in a new way that attracts customers.

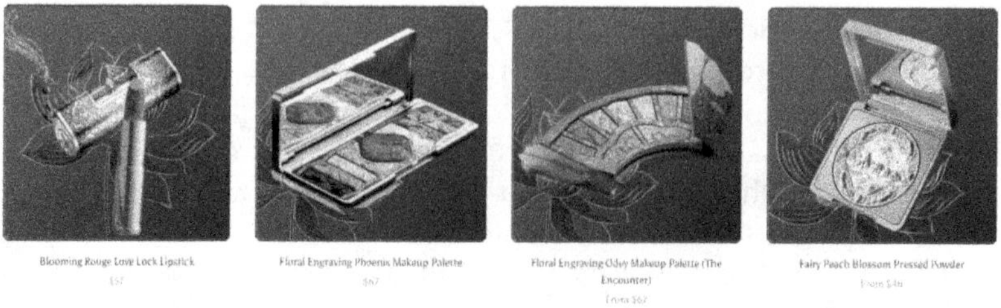

Screenshot of Florasis website showcasing different products

Since its establishment, each product launched by Florasis has adopted classical elements in packaging and names, allowing the brand concept of "Oriental Makeup, Makeup with Flowers" to penetrate into the hearts of consumers.

For a long time, Florasis, a domestic cosmetics product, has conveyed to consumers the image of an oriental classical beauty. Today, this image has been presented more three-dimensionally. On June 1 2021, Florasis officially released the first virtual image "Florasis" on its official account, giving a face to a name.

“Florasis” is pictured as a young woman exhibiting graceful retro makeup, lotus leaf earrings, wearing a lotus leaf dress.

The birth of brand avatars, without exception, is a means for brands to attract young people. Through a more fashionable and trendy virtual image, it attracts the attention of young consumers and establishes a deeper emotional communication with consumers.

There are many benefits of virtual avatars. First, no marketing team will be needed to pick and choose which celebrity would best embody the brand, since the full avatar is created by the design team. Second, there has been recent celebrity scandals that has derailed the image of the celebrity so much so that brands have cancelled their contracts. For instance, several brands cancelled their contracts immediately with Kris Wu, who was deemed to have sexual misconduct with minors. Virtual avatars will never fall prey to scandals and every word and representation can be controlled by the brand. Third, it is very easy to insert avatars in ads in a fast-developing meta world dominated by virtual reality.

But the downsides also cannot be forgotten. After all, virtual images are not real characters and cannot interact with consumers on their own. Instead, a team of people needs to operate behind the scenes of the brand. Once the brand begins slacking in character maintenance, the connection between the virtual image and consumers will be interrupted.

Blind Boxes and the Hook Model

During my time working in the Tmall Overseas team, I was able to see the success of many Chinese brands entering foreign markets and the increasing stickiness it had that differentiated them from local players. This led me to study one brand in particular in much greater detail, a toy brand by the name of Popmart.

When Popmart CEO, Wang Ning, was a child, his parents worked in a shop selling videos, clocks, fishing gear and other gadgets. Most of his childhood and spare time was spent in his parents' shop.

Every day, all kinds of customers came to the store to buy things, so Wang Ning unknowingly had a strong interest in business, something that ultimately would inspire his own venture in the business world.

In 2005 in university, Wang Ning's first business idea was to record shots of student life and burn them into CDs. Soon these CDs became popular among classes and campuses, and many students asked him to burn them. He realized that since most students would rather watch a documentary on their own life, his next step was to shoot personalized videos. When the new freshmen entered the school, Wang Ning established a club called "Days Studio" and started his own business.

They would film freshmen registering at school, the welcome party, various club activities, and networking activities, the first batch of 1,000 CDs produced were sold out in one day. Wang Ning and the "Days Studio" team quickly became popular that later became a full-fledged studio, but as web streaming took hold in China, CD's were less and less popular. The business eventually died out but gave Wang enough hope to venture into his next business.

Wang Ning took the existing team to investigate Hangzhou and Yiwu and purchased some interesting small wares such as toys and home goods and sold them. It was there that they came across an emerging retail format called the "Grid Shop" in early 2008. These stores gathered all kinds of products, stationery, cameras, pillows, stuffed animals. They're basically the real life version of what Muji or Miniso is today without the unified branding.

The grid shop had a low threshold for opening a store, which invited many competitors later on. The most difficult part was controlling the quality of products, the growing number of SKUs and low profit margin.

When Wang Ning was distraught at this stage as an entrepreneur, a doll called Sonny Angel entered the scene.

Product photo of the Chinese Zodiac Series of Pop Mart

This doll is a hand-made ornament about 3 inches tall with hundreds of styles. Wang Ning decided to place these toys in identical packaging. This was the birth of the "blind box". As a customer, you didn't know which doll you would be getting. This later fueled a frenzy in that some customers would spend hundreds of dollars to find the doll that he or she wanted. Toy collectors dove deeper into the trend to collect all the available dolls in a series. For instance, pictured above is the Chinese Zodiac series. This was the core piece that fueled Popmart's success.

Fast forward to present day, offline Popmart vending machines are ubiquitous in access for customers to purchase toys from different shopping malls. This allowed Wang's physical retail to be reduced as some stores are simply "pop up" stores (pun intended) of vending machines.

Photo of a Pop mart vending machine

Sales have soared from a few thousand a month to tens of thousands a month, and this number is still rising. Many limited editions are sold out. Popmart became the Toys R Us for adults.

Now, the figurines have evolved into all kinds of collaborations from Harry Potter to Hello Kitty. What later transpired was a rapid design model that can be compared to the likes of Zara in the fast fashion world. Popmart became the Zara in the collectible toys world.

Soon, Wang entered Tmall to provide an omnichannel experience for his customers, differentiating the online store to have some figurines only available online, forcing his fans to shop from the online store as well.

Popmart's Tmall Flagship store featuring a new series Bobo & Coco

Recently, Bubble Mart was listed on the Hong Kong Stock Exchange. It rose by 79.22% on the first day of trading in a roughly $600 million dollar IPO.

Blind Boxes and the Hook Model

Today, the blind box concept in China has seeped into various sectors including food and travel items. For instance, for those who are indecisive as to what to order for food delivery for lunch can opt into a Blind Box meal, where the contents are not revealed until the consumer opens the box. In terms of travel, consumers can also hop on a tour with an airline but not know which destination the airline will ultimately pick. My most recent sighting of blind box was in dating, in which a single bachelor can choose various filters to then select a potential date (think Tinder without the photos) to then arrive at a formal group date event to meeting his selection.

Grenade燃拓健康食品
GRENADE 燃拓
小红书盲盒尝新活动
盲盒计划
(6支装)
限时抽奖 | 立即参与
双11宠粉专属 | Grenade6只装盲盒尝新来啦！！
巧克力布朗尼，黑巧树莓，海盐焦糖……
哪一个是你本命？？总有宝宝说一次性买12支太多啦，想有尝新包装。这不就给大家安排上了！
2090
2074
279

Screenshot from Little Red Book on a Blind Box for granola bars

Consumers today need to be evermore stimulated and entertained. The Blind Box concept was one such experiment that was tested and later became successful. I predict that this will be one of many marketing gimmicks that will arise from the Chinese consumer market.

When I first heard of the blind box concept, I immediately thought of a book I had read years ago on product development. Several years ago, I had come upon Nir Eyal's Hood Model and observed the pattern of how the Hook Model stretches into several successful apps and products.

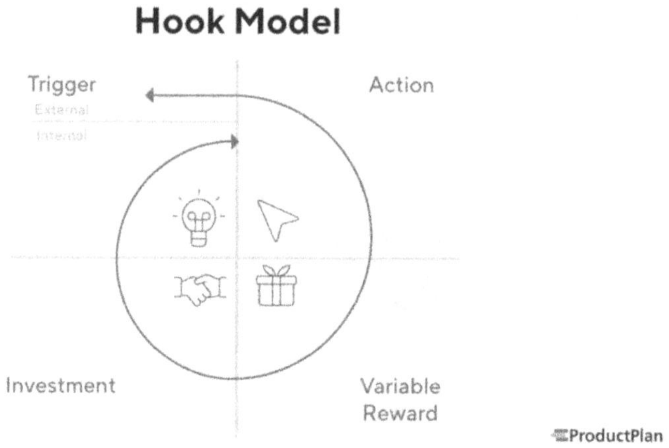

Nir Eyal's Hood Model Diagram

The Hook Model posits that every successful product was "sticky" enough to retain its users and achieve growth because of these four principles: action, variable reward (this part is key), investment and trigger.

Trigger: A 'trigger' is an instigator of behavior and comes in two types, external and internal. An external trigger is one that is external to you, the user. An internal trigger is one that is internal to you such as hunger, sleepiness, irritation etc.

Action: The behavior done in anticipation of a reward.

Variable Reward: A changing reward mechanism whether in amount, existence or other that answers to the pain point for the user. The variability part is what makes them come back, again and again.

Investment: The repetition of the previous three steps eventually accumulates in a form of investment for the user, increasing stickiness for the user to continue to return.

When a potential customer for Popmart sees the ubiquitous vending machines of Popmart littered in Chinese malls, they are faced with an external trigger. Or, when their friends have uncovered a coveted doll that they have not yet added to their collected, there is an internal trigger happening by way of envy. Their next action is to act in a way that would solve their pain point by purchasing the item. However, they are next met with a variable reward since they do not know which doll they will get until opening the box. Finally, as they accumulate more dolls, they subconsciously add to their roster of dolls, thereby emphasizing the collection further. This cycle will then continue to repeat itself, paving way for a successful brand.

VR, AR

In 2016, Tmall did try to introduce VR into shopping. At the Detroit Gateway conference, a roadshow for western audiences, we enabled attendees to play with our VR product. Back then I had not formally joined Alibaba yet, but we enabled attendees to put on VR googles and navigate a living room where they can explore different types of products and click into entering different rooms. However, most Chinese families still did not have VR goggles, and thus the product lost steam thereafter.

In 2020 though, perhaps because of the epidemic, the team had to find new and innovative ways for consumers to experience products even at home. Today, AR became the answer. While some thought that luxury products could not be successful in ecommerce because of the price tag of each item, Tmall actually proved them wrong. Tools like AR Try On are enabling users to start to experiment with the brand or product that they otherwise wouldn't be able to. We've all been there, not really wanting to enter a luxury store because of the icy cold stares from sales associates or just the annoyance of a sales associate chasing you around the store. Sometimes we just want to look at products by ourselves! Now with AR try on, you can!

I would argue this might even trump going to the physical store. Imagine if you wanted to buy a watch. Do you have the time or the energy to go to every single luxury watch brand? Or is it more convenient to do a few taps on your iPhone and slap the different watches on your wrist?

Last year, the same function was opened for shoes and sunglasses. I predict this will be a fast-rising trend and possible be ready for clothing in the future as well.

In the category of cosmetics, this is taking greater strides in having the customer experiment with the product. Taking trying on lipstick for example. While at the store, you have the physical product being put on you with an object that has been used on everyone else, then if the color does not work, you must wash it off and reapply. With AR try on, you can try as many colors on your face as you want by simply clicking on other brands and colors.

VR shopping still has some time to catch up, mostly dependent on the ubiquity of having VR goggles. This extra piece of hardware is not easy to distribute and thus, this piece might be a while away.

Works Cited

Alibaba. (2020). *Alibaba investor relations reports*. https://www.alibabagroup.com/en/ir/presentations/Investor_Day_2020_AlibabaDigital.pdf

Bloomberg News. (2020). *The World's livestream queen can sell anything*. https://www.bloomberg.com/features/2020-viya-china-livestream-shopping/

Canaves, S. (2019). *How L'oreal won single's day*. China Film Insider. https://chinafilminsider.com/loreal-singles-day

Chi, R. (2021). *Why China's blind box economy is a good bet for brands*. https://www.thedrum.com/opinion/2021/10/20/why-china-s-blind-box-economy-good-bet-brands

CNN. (2021). *Chinese millennials are not getting married and the government is worried*. Here's Why. Retrieved from: https://www.news18.com/news/buzz/changing-attitudes-is-causing-chinese-millennials-to-not-get-married-and-the-government-is-worried-3368438.html

Eyal, N., & Hoover, R. (2014). *Hooked: How to build habit-forming products*.

Greenwald, M. (2020). *Live streaming e-commerce is the rage in china*. Is The U.S. Next? https://www.forbes.com/sites/michellegreenwald/2020/12/10/live-streaming-e-commerce-is-the-rage-in-china-is-the-us-next/?sh=64928c246535

Kling, M. (2021). *Qualityland*.

Nierynck, R. (2020). *Delivery hero*. https://www.deliveryhero.com/blog/quick-commerce/

Xinhuanet (2017). *Women dominate higher education in China*. http://www.xinhuanet.com/english/2017-10/27/c_136710572.htm

Yau, E. (2020). *Toymaker pop mart on a tear: US$674 million IPO came a decade after first store opened in Beijing*. SCMP. https://www.scmp.com/lifestyle/entertainment/article/3114778/toymaker-pop-mart-tear-us674-million-ipo-came-decade-after

Zhang, P. (2021). *Ad showing woman avoid sexual assault by using make-up remover withdrawn after it causes outrage online*. SCMP. https://www.scmp.com/news/people-culture/trending-china/article/3117284/ad-showing-woman-avoid-sexual-assault-using-make

CHAPTER 4

Application

Case Studies

Branding in China is something that has bubbled up recently coinciding with the advent of the internet. When I was growing up, most of the brands that I consumed were owned by SOE's or state-owned-enterprises. From the milk that I drank in the morning, to the clothing that I wore to the toys that I played with, a lot of products I touched as a child were unbranded, or brandless. This was because China, a country that was ripe with labor and manufacturing, was good at producing instead of telling a brand story. Fast forward two decades, with the advent of Taobao, this has become something different recently.

I will be sharing a couple of examples that have truly made a mark in the ecommerce space and set a new standard within a certain category. Each brand is impressive because each one developed its competitive advantage and made it a differentiator in the market, paving the way for its strategy to be replicated by other brands to be applied in another category of products. The below will be the framework that I will be using to introduce each brand and what made them tick in the world's most competitive market.

S. Gai, *Ecommerce Reimagined*,
https://doi.org/10.1007/978-981-19-0003-7_4

Brand:
Achievement:
What made it work:

These will appear at the beginning of every brand story so that readers can also have a quick snapshot of what worked and didn't work. You will notice that not only am I describing each case's good sides, but I am also telling the bad sides as well and the lessons that can be learned from each case. Just like companies, no venture is always smooth sailing and successful from day one, but the ebb and flow of each brand paves way for new entrants to emerge to fairly have a chance at making a mark on the market.

Case Study: Perfect Diary, a Lesson in "Explosive Marketing"

Brand: Perfect Diary
Achievement: Revenue size of 800 million RMB in 5 years
What made it work: Tiered usage of KOLs and creative crossover products

The day that I left Perfect Diary's office on one sunny afternoon in Guangzhou, I definitely felt old. Throughout the meeting, no matter if it was the front desk or the people that brought me water or the people in the meeting looked no more than 25 years old.

Perfect Diary is a home-grown cosmetics brand launched in 2017, a brand that was later studied by various cosmetics brands from global players liked L'oreal to smaller domestic players. It was the brand that emerged out of nowhere and one that took over the category by storm.

Perfect Diary's parent company is Yatsen Holding recently went public on the NASDAQ after three years of starting the brand. Yatsen, based out of Guangzhou, also owns other brands such as Abby's Choice and Little Ondine. It recently acquired Eve Lom which is a foreign brand from Britain.

What is their secret to explosive growth?

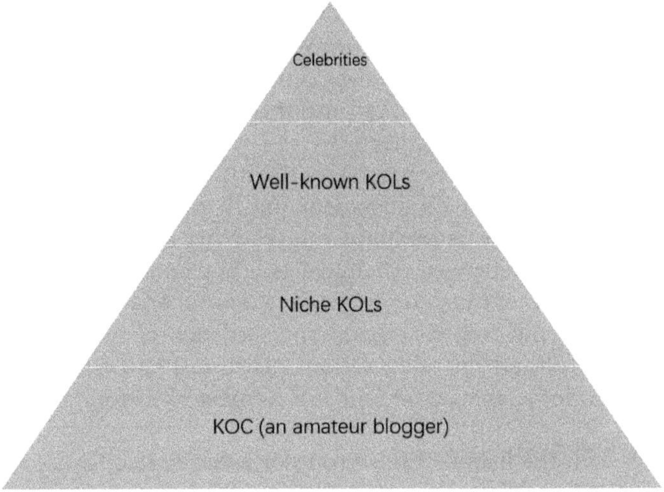

Perfect Diary used a pyramid model for its launch strategy. As of January 2020, the number of fans of Perfect Diary on Little Red Book is 1.7 million, which is much higher than that of other European, American or domestic beauty brands (for example, L'Oreal has only 180,000 fans at the time of writing).

The launch of Perfect Diary on Little Red Book can be seen as a pyramid model created by a combination of celebrities, well-known KOLs, niche KOLs, and KOC (an amateur blogger). At the top of the layout pyramid, Perfect Diary first invests in celebrity endorsements and the promotion of well-known KOLs to create a brand image benchmark. The celebrity endorsement is a kind of endorsement, which can arouse the initial attention and discussion of niche KOLs to also start following the brand. However, the bigger focus is to put the mid-range KOLs and amateur KOLs or even KOCs to the test. This batch of users mainly uses product reviews as content exposure to plant a seed for their friends to purchase later.

Finally, because Perfect Diary in the previous steps has formed a natural trend and traffic on Little Red Book, ordinary consumers will create content and share on the platform again after purchase, forming a secondary dissemination, forming a healthy flow cycle.

Why is this delivery strategy effective?

The target audience of Perfect Diary is mostly students born after 1995 and 2000. The characteristic of this target group is that their growth is accompanied by the development of electronic products and social networks, and at the same time they are at the age of pursuing individuality and personal opinions.

This group of people have natural sensitivity and vigilance to "advertising". Having grown up with documentaries that expose the dark side of marketing, they are not as traditional in receiving advertisement as their boomer parents or millennial counterparts. They don't buy into authoritative endorsements as much or direct ads from the brand. They are more inclined to trust the true evaluation and feedback of other consumers, and they are proficient in using various platforms, know how to search for product reviews, and do all kinds of homework before purchasing a product.

Familiar with the habits of this group of users, Perfect Diary aimed at Little Red Book early on. More than 80% of LRB users are young women, focused on content on makeup, skin care, and fashion. At the same time, everyone posts notes, and even amateur notes are more popular with users and easier to get traffic.

It's in this platform that Perfect Diary makes full use of the many-to-many communication model, where multiple consumers (from amateurs to KOLs to celebrities) recommends products to multiple consumers.

Private domain traffic is a popular concept in marketing in recent years. In fact, it is the traffic that bloggers can control by themselves. The most common forms are WeChat, WeChat groups, small programs, or autonomous apps.

The private domain traffic of Perfect Diary is not as strong as its presence on Little Red Book, but it is well laid out and has brought a lot of conversion. Its private domain traffic diversion mainly comes from two channels:

Perfect Diary opened more than 30 offline experience stores in 19 years, and the power of transforming traffic from offline to online brought by these stores cannot be ignored. For example, the offline experience store of Perfect Diary in Guangzhou has a daily traffic of about 2,000 people. The counter workers of the experience store will guide customers to the store to add a WeChat account of Perfect Diary as friends called Xiaowanzi. Xiaowanzi is an avatar created by Perfect Diary to represent their brand in a more personable, human form.

Xiaowanzi is not only a customer service, but also a very three-dimensional image. Her WeChat group is dominated by lucky draws, live broadcasts and other activities, and there are many beauty tutorials. This content has increased consumers' interest and frequency of interaction, and made consumers feel that the brand cares about themselves as an individual.

Another strategy that has continued Perfect Diary's branding to its consumers is their collaboration projects. The advantage of a crossover product is to bring together the popularity and traffic enthusiasm of the two brands to create a win-win situation. At the same time, the cross-border gimmick arouses the curiosity of consumers, thereby bringing greater volume and discussion, enhancing marketing effects.

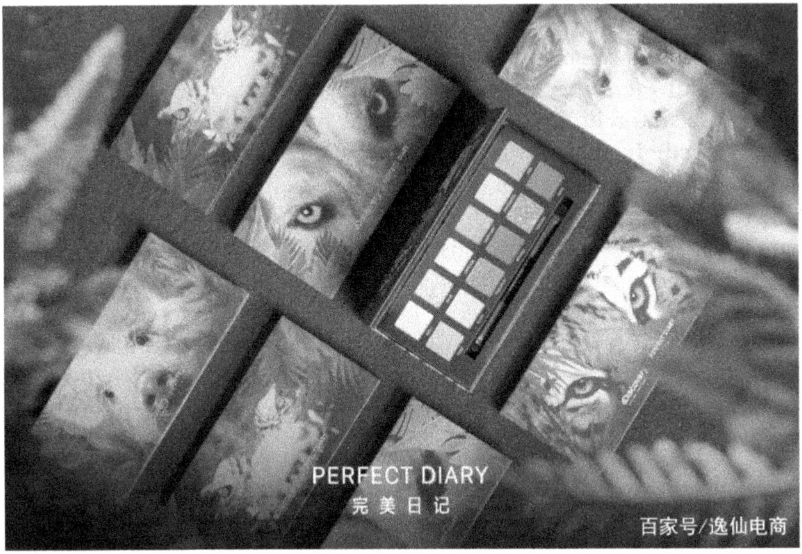

Perfect Diaryís Animal eyeshadow plate jointly marketed with Discovery Channel

The Animal Eyeshadow Palette is a twelve-color eye shadow product jointly launched by Perfect Diary and Discovery Channel. When this product launched, the brand chose 4 KOLs, each catering to a niche makeup group. There are several different pallets to choose from such as the Piggy pallete, the Crocodile pallete, the Kitten or Puppy pallete (My favorite has been the Kitten pallete!).

For example, @小猪姐which has 5 million Weibo fans endorses the Piggy Pallet. Her appearance is more gentle and sweet, and she often does imitation makeup from Japan and South Korea.

The spokesperson of the Crocodile plate is Vivekatt, who has 1 million Weibo fans. Although her fans are not as many as the other spokespersons (all over 2.5 million fans), Vivekatt likes to wear bright, colorful makeup, so her fans are very precise people who like this atypical Asian makeup.

The main consumers of Perfect Diary are young people who pursue individuality rather than what was heralded by the ideals of their previous generation. They have evolved into a generation pursuing personalization. Therefore, the choice of "Discovery Channel" used as an element for co-branding met the needs of this group of people for integration of personality and culture.

Yatsen, the mother company of Perfect Diary, is wishing to replicate this success to its other brands. They are evolving to become an ecommerce accelerator housing several beauty brands that are both organic and acquired. In conclusion, Perfect Diary's success is mainly focused on their organized usage of KOLs, tiering them in different categories and creating an explosive effect of permeating the product to their target market. Their new collaborations with content channels that is followed by their target market renews the "freshness" of the brand with their audience. Finally, their usage of wielding the "private sphere of traffic" to have a customer service agent to speak on a one on one basis with their customers is what retains the stickiness of the brand. I'm excited to see the future brands this ecommerce accelerator is evolving into.

Case Study: Adopt-a-Cow, a New Sales Model in CPG

Brand: Adopt-a-Cow
Achievement: Revenue size of 2 billion and becoming number one brand in Tmall Dairy, surpassing the two major incumbents in three years
What made it work: its unique business model in breaking into a traditional industry

In 2012, Xu Xiaobo went to Hong Kong and bought eight cans of milk powder for his baby. But when he passed the Hong Kong Customs, because the quantity of milk powder exceeded the prescribed 2 cans that was allowed for a single consumer purchase, he was detained in a small black room for 4 hours.

After coming back to China, he decided he wanted to raise his own cows and milk his own milk. This was the start of Adopt-a-Cow, an internet milk brand that quickly rose to fame in 2018.

The dairy industry, like any traditional industry, had been cemented for years by two major players. In this case, they were Mengniu and Yili, both dairy giants that have gone on to sponsor the Olympics. Naturally, they were the two dominant brands in Tmall as well. The year that I had joined Tmall in 2018 was when the scoreboard still had these two in the lead. A couple of years later, however, Adopt-a-Cow came out number one. During Tmall Double 11 in 2020, the Adopt-a-Cow sold more than 100 million yuan, and it became the number one dairy product flagship store.

How did this dairy brand do it?

Through an innovative sales model that was able to amass a huge number of consumers, quickly. It's also evident in the name: adoption.

The first type is cloud adoption, which is equivalent to cloud-raising cats and cloud-raising dogs. Users can use Taobao or WeChat mini-programs and play a game that "raise" cattle, similar to the game of raising a Tamagotchi Pet and watch the live broadcasts of the ranch.

The second is joint adoption. Users can purchase seasonal, semi-annual, and annual membership cards, and enjoy a subscription product year-round.

The third type is real-name adoption, that is, to become a true cattle-raising partner. This requires users to reserve milk one year in advance at the exclusive ranch. The highest-ranking members can also name the cows, and Adopt-a-Cow will regularly send you the cow's photos and various growth data to the owner.

This model was inspired by a similar investment case for Yunfang Tea Garden. As a high-end private tea garden in China, Yunfang has a coveted garden of 30,000 acres in Mount Emei. These small tea gardens are sold to users with a 5-year right to harvest from the land and users can obtain a certain amount of tea produced by this tea garden every year.

The cloud release model can also be said to be "adopting a tea garden." Thus, this is an easy model to apply to also vineyards.

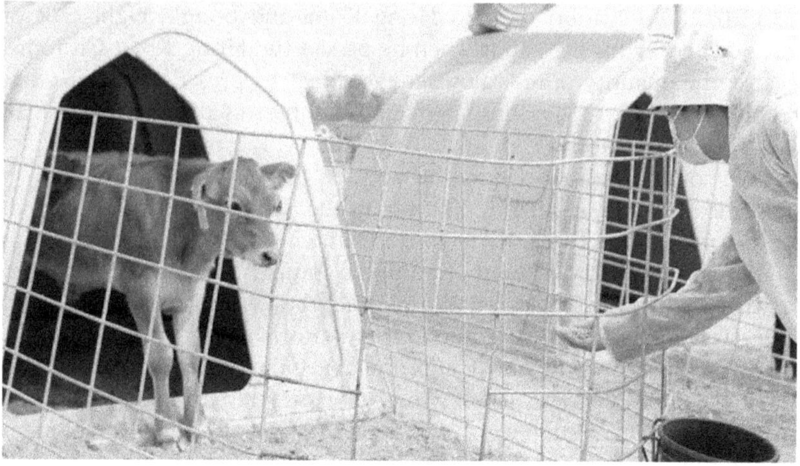

Photo of Adopt-a-Cow farm

The model of Adopt-a-Cow is similar to the business model of a traditional offline service provider such as a barber shop. Members are required to purchase a card, usually in a large lump sum amount, which enables the member to get X amount of dollars as a gift. This allows the offline service provider to quickly amass a large cash number into its account, which immediately offsets large offline investments.

In order to attract more people to apply for adoption cards, Adopt-a-Cow has also recruited ambassadors and opened affiliate marketing, playing out the concepts of "cow-raising partner". Say if you became an ambassador that you then sold to a friend, you can potentially earn 15% in commission.

Does this model sound familiar? Mary Kay functioned in the same way. In fact, this sort of program can apply to any sort of product.

The dairy industry is a red ocean industry. When a user walks to a convenience store and wants to buy a pack of milk, he hardly thinks about the choice between Brand X and Y. Whichever brand was closer to the fridge door is the one that was drunk in the end. This is very similar to the competition between Coca-Cola and Pepsi. For these instant consumer goods, the hardest problem to tackle is how to get closer to the consumer.

Many regional milk brands have even installed a milk box at the door of every household. As long as the user makes a reservation, he can definitely drink the freshest milk the first time he gets up every morning. So the only way Adopt-a-cow can win from this type of competitor is if they are able to have more customers join into the adoption system. Now, Adopt-a-Cow online sales account for about 70% of its total sales. From the perspective of the entire dairy industry, online channels account for less than 10%. This is where Adopt-a-Cow is winning.

Is this a marketing trick? Absolutely! This dairy brand has just figured out a new way to crack into a rigid traditional industry. But the concept is working. In an age where consumers want to know with more vehemence where their food is coming from, a brand that emphasizes traceability is definitely on a good path to win.

Case Study: Liziqi, a Lesson in Traffic Monetization

Brand: 李子柒 Liziqi
Achievement: A Youtube channel that eventually became a household brand name in the food industry
What made it work: impeccable and unique content that enlivens traditional farm products into a contemporary brand

"No matter how much I love modern technology, I can't restrain my yearning for this kind of life. She seems to be able to make every part of the crop into a delicacy. She really wants to have the same recipes, and she also wants to understand the traditional Chinese culture in the video."

"I have been suffering from depression for four years. Watching this girl's video, I can always find peace of mind. When the popcorn exploded, she and the puppy screamed in fright, and it made me feel full of life's fireworks."

"The little things she took care of her grandma always reminded me of my hometown, childhood, and parents. Thank you for the video. Please keep shooting."

These are the comments that one can find below Liziqi's Youtube videos.

A photo of Liziqi in her home

Almost mythical in nature, and shot with mesmerizing countryside cinematography, Liqizi is a Sichuan girl born in the 90's from a poor family. She was brought up in the mountains by her grandparents. She started working out at the age of fourteen. She worked as a waiter in a restaurant and a bar DJ. Later, she returned to take care of her sick grandmother. After returning home, Li Ziqi opened an online shop. She started to shoot short videos because she wanted to diversify her business. As a result, the online shop was not popular and the video became popular.

Li rarely speaks in her videos, instead it's the sounds of nature, cooking, and calm music that dominate the video. One magazine described her videos to be an ASMR trance. "The only narration is friendly banter between Li and her grandmother, but the sounds—the singing of birds, the crunch of frost underfoot, the thwack of a cleaver, the sizzle of frying garlic—lure you into an ASMR trance."

Among the many domestic and foreign content platforms it operates, the revenue from YouTube is the most substantial. Li Ziqi's 100 videos on YouTube have a total of 2 billion views, with an average of 25 million views per video, and the most popular one has nearly 100 million views. According to Nox Influencer's forecast, Li Ziqi's annual income through the YouTube platform's traffic sharing can be as high as 40 million RMB.

In just a few years, Li Ziqi took traditional Chinese food culture as the subject, through her beautiful archaic lens and rural narrative approach, showing a series of pastoral sceneries that are different from the fast-paced life of the concrete jungle, who are asking for an escape from their urban lives.

In September 2016, Li Ziqi received a private message from a MCN organization called Weinian, wishing to sign with her. A MCN organization is an entity similar to an agent company that has contracts with celebrities to manage them. It makes money by incubating KOLs to become Internet celebrities.

Using the fans accumulated on the video platform as the source of traffic, Li Ziqi's Tmall flagship store of the same name officially opened in August 2018. It was Weinian who helped Liziqi develop packaged products of the dishes she would make in her videos. Suddenly, her viewers were able to purchase things that they would watch daily on her videos.

In 2019, the total annual sales of Li Ziqi's Tmall flagship store was 71 million yuan. The epidemic in 2020 accelerated the development of e-commerce, and the annual sales of Li Ziqi's flagship store reached 1 billion yuan. Products mostly include snail noodles, purple sweet potato steamed rice cakes, and lotus root noodles, all of which are still very popular products today. Snail noodles, now an extremely popular dish in China, doesn't have snails in them (at least her version doesn't). However, the stinky smell from the noodles seems to be what the fans are craving, similar to the craze of the stinky tofu as a street food favorite in Hunan.

Relying on the fan traffic on overseas platforms, Li Ziqi IP later expanded into an independent cross-border e-commerce site. The products on its platform are different from Tmall brand stores, which mainly focus on food,. surrounding traditional Chinese clothing accessories, kitchenware, and handicrafts.

Today, her products can be found in almost every supermarket in China as the online brand has also successfully anchored itself in offline markets.

Case Study: Neiwai, Changing China's Perception on Beauty

Brand: NEIWAI (Translated: Inside Out)
Achievement: A new definition of being body positive in China for the lingerie industry
What made it work: differentiation in marketing content

NEIWAI has made a splash in China's lingerie market by defying the traditional beauty standards that has always favored thin girls and push-up bras in exchange for acceptance of all body types and comfort and simplicity. The look of the Victoria's Secret Angel was also the dominant image selling lingerie in China for many years. Neiwai took away the metal structure inside the bra in priority for the comfort of the woman. The product design of these brands also speaks to the lifestyle preferences of younger women. Neiwai commits itself to fighting ageism and sizeism.

NEIWAI, translated means Inside and Outside. The brand's founder purports that the "Nei-" of Neiwai means the "Inside" represents the heart and acceptance of all emotions that enter the heart. The "-wai" of Neiwai is the "Outside" represents the body and acceptance of the beauty of multiple bodies. The brand name has established NEIWAI's brand feelings of always focusing on "people" inside and outside, encouraging women to liberate their bodies and return to themselves.

NEIWAI has been called a brand that is like a "love letter to women". From the products, the aesthetics of design, the high quality of the fabrics, the persistence of comfort to the content creation in stores, all portray what the brand stands for, a change in the lingerie space.

In 2012, the consumers of NEIWAI are "a group of pioneer women with overseas education background and confidence about their bodies. They are young and mature, and may already be mothers, so they have higher requirements for the comfort of underwear." But in the past few years, brand users have gradually diversified and become younger. The 18–25 year old customer base has grown from 25% in 2017 to 37% in 2019. This generation of young people embraces the brand's marketing ethos calling acceptance of multiple bodies, so they have a high sense of identity with the brand concept of NEIWAI.

Recently, global pop star, Faye Wong, was picked for the brand as the brand's global spokesperson, who echoes the personality of the brand, with a free and unrestrained avant-garde expression in music, fashion, film, and life. Slowly, what was originally an underwear brand has transformed itself into a full-category intimate clothing lifestyle brand. NEIWAI has expanded into pajamas, home wear, casual clothes and most recently launched into the sportswear market.

Perhaps their most successful product line is the "Zero Min" series, which has been very popular until now. The rise of this product series has a lot to do with the feminist trend of liberating the body and pursuing freedom at that time.

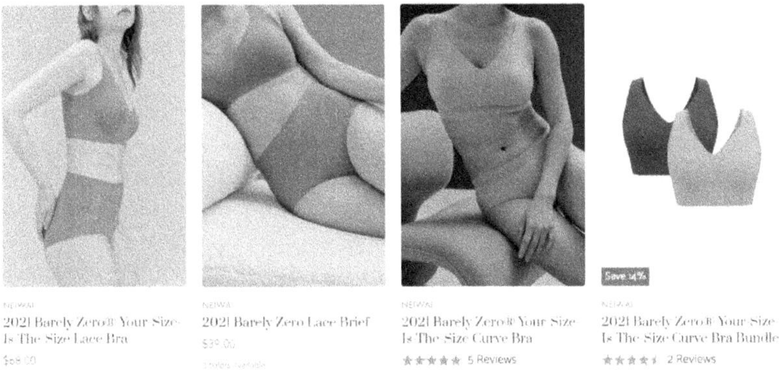

Product photos from Neiwaiís website

NEIWAI began its physical store settlement in first-tier malls such as Kerry Center and Swire to establish a mid-to-high-end brand image and a solid retail positioning, and then gradually opening in mid range malls.

NEIWAI also attracted a group of women unexpectedly, the LBGT, gay, bisexual, and transgender group who had different needs of wanting tighter bras to restrain their bodies and make their breasts look smaller. Since diversity was always at the core of their brand, the NEIWAI product team is constantly looking at how to evolve fabrics to accommodate for their different niche user groups.

Case Study: Zihaiguo, an Attempt to Replace Instant Noodles

Brand: 自嗨锅 ZHG Self Heating Hot Pot
Achievement: Revenue size of 100 million USD within 3 years
What made it work: understanding the needs of the target market and capturing the trend of the "lazy economy" early

Purchasing instant noodles to a Chinese family is like a family saving up on toilet paper during a pandemic. It's considered an essential part of the cupboard, a basic staple that is consumed. With China consuming 44 billion units annually, this is one of the largest food segments in China.

I had met the team of ZHG in a food conference in 2018, a year after the brand was launched. Dressed in all black, head to toe, the Brand Director looked like someone from an Alexander Wang fashion show runway. It was a food industry conference, riveted with industry experts from consulting companies with fancy powerpoint slides. When it was ZHG's turn to go up, the team showed three slides in succession in black background and blood red letters in a comical font. The slides read: Fun, Young, Easy.

"Zi Hai Guo, Zi Hai Guo, one person can eat Zi Hai Guo", the magic song of ZHG resounded in all major buildings and shopping malls in 2018. You could see ZHG in live broadcast rooms and entertainment programs of major broadcasters.

A product that has been quite common in Japan, but hardly so in western countries consists of a two layered product in which the bottom layer contains a packet that heats up when cold water is poured over. By closing the lid of the top layer, the steam generated from the bottom layer heats the top layer, containing the food. ZHG has made several dishes already, and some contain rice. Steamed rice in 15 minutes, no rice cooker or electricity necessary. The only external ingredient was cold water. Its mascot is an astronaut dog, claiming ZHG is the food of the spacemen.

Instant noodles used to be the king of instant food, but even that had required hot water, which can be hard to access at times. This way of "cooking" hit very close to home for the Gen Z generation that had little cooking skills and little patience to spend time in making meals.

This young brand, established less than three years ago, has become popular at a very fast speed, and has influenced half of the entertainment circle, becoming the representative of the current Internet celebrity brand.

Perhaps the biggest and most correct insight from Cai's part was his intuition of the current trend. The word 宅 in Chinese, which means house, has evolved, in recent years, into an adjective to describe people who prefer to stay at home. Coupled with a delay in marriage, there are many young people who are single. "At home and single" might sound a little unfortunate in the western context, it is all the norm in a Chinese one.

According to CBN Data's "2018 Consumer Trends Report", the number of users of the food delivery service App under the age of 24 has increased by more than 10 million, contributing 44% of the growth. Other data show that in 2018, China's single population has reached 260 million, of which more than 77 million adults are living alone.

"At home and single", a new lifestyle for contemporary young people has fueled a new lane to develop within the fast food industry and ZHG has been the biggest winner so far.

Where there is a market, there is competition. Up to now, hundreds of brands have entered the market. On the self-heating hot pot, there are not only emerging brands such as Zihai Pot, but also well-known hot pot brands such as Haidilao.

Although Zihai Pot is not the first company to enter the market to make self-heating food, it has seized the minds of users through advertising slogans such as "Not all self-heating hot pots are Zihai Pots". Nowadays, many consumers are searching for "what brand of self-heating pot is delicious". In the minds of consumers, the brand of Zihai Pot is in the lead.

In 2018, the products went online and achieved sales of over 100 million yuan in just three quarters. In 2019, sales reached nearly 800 million yuan. The epidemic became another blessing in disguise. With people on lockdown, supply chain in fresh food was gravely affected which caused ZHG to increase by more than 200%. In the first half of 2020, Zihaiguo's sales performance has reached 600 million yuan.

There are currently nearly 200 SKUs, including hot pot, claypot rice, spicy hot pot. In the future, they are venturing into hot dry noodles, Chongqing noodles and other products.

Perhaps the biggest differentiation on ZHG's marketing is the change in context of where the brand is used. Do you remember the last leg of the Triangle we discussed of People, Product and Context? ZHG narrowed its product down to four "scenes": home, work, leisure places, and outdoors. When planting the product in these different spaces, ZHG pictures the consumer fully enjoying the product. The goal is to have the consumer think about the self-heating hot pot product when they are in that context.

During the pandemic, livestream was also hugely in ZHG's favor. Because of the different steps in the product, a demonstration on the product allowed for more air time versus a product that has less "layers". As potential consumers watched as top KOLs opened the packaging to reveal the water, the rice, the sauces, the meat, and adding each packet one by one added to the product. Similar to what Betty Crocker had one in modern marketing when it came to selling cake mix where the consumer has the illusion of "cooking", ZHG did the same to a clay pot rice dish or a hot pot. By opening each packet, and pouring water, the consumer is also under the illusion of "cooking".

Case Study: Saturn Bird, Intertwining Sustainability and Coffee

Brand: 三顿半 Saturn Bird Coffee
Achievement: 62 million USD in 5 years, opening first offline location in 2021
What made it work: developing a freeze dried version of coffee that consumers found more convenient than freshly brewed coffee

China is traditionally a tea market. Chinese consumers drink nine times more tea than coffee. But that is slowly changing, especially amongst the young urbanites in Tier 1 cities. Set at approximately 14 billion USD, the coffee industry in China is still growing at 10% a year.

Saturn Bird product photos

Saturn Bird Coffee was founded in Changsha in 2015, and its products are mainly freeze-dried instant coffee in small cups. Unlike traditional instant coffee that only dissolves in hot water, freeze-dried coffee powder can be dissolved in cold water and milk, which is more convenient and retains more flavor of coffee.

In the Double 11 of 2021, Saturn Bird ranked number 1 in sales in the coffee category, larger than any traditional instant coffee brand such as Nescafe or Maxwell.

Before founding Saturn Bird Coffee, however, the founder, Wu Jun had opened an offline cafe in Changsha for eight years. This offline chain did not scale anywhere near to the capacity that an online brand could. This is what led him to Saturn Bird Coffee. His biggest problem to overcome was whether the product can compete with fresh brew in a physical coffee store, which was always thought to taste better than instant coffee.

Freeze-drying, technically, is not a new technology, but the "combination of convenience and quality" is in line with user habits under the trend of popularization of coffee culture. By 2021, even freshly ground coffee brands have also launched freeze-dried coffee products, such as K Café of KFC.

Transaction volume, average annual compound growth rate, repurchase rate, gross profit margin and customer acquisition cost are keys to measurement for the health of an online brand.

High gross profit means relatively large room for marketing expenses. Wu Jun considered marketing a little differently than his traditional coffee counterparts, involving a sustainability element instead. In 2019, Saturn Bird Coffee opened a recycling plan where users can return empty coffee cans. The user can take the empty can to the cooperating offline boutique coffee shop at a specified time to redeem new coffee and merchandise. On Double 11 that year, the transaction volume of the flagship store of Saturn Bird Coffee surpassed Nestlé Coffee for the first time.

Wu Jun said that the sales of Saturn Bird Coffee in the first half of 2021 had exceeded that of 2020, and the revenue of Saturn Bird Coffee in 2020 is nearly 400 million yuan. In the past three years, Saturn Bird Coffee has basically maintained a two-to-three-time annual growth rate, with a repurchase rate of nearly 50%.

The size of China's coffee market is predicted to increase to 144.7 billion RMB by 2025. However, Tmall's instant coffee sales last year was only about 5 billion RMB, which means there is still a lot of room for growth.

After a successful launch on Tmall, this internet brand is now considering opening offline retail locations.

Since 2020, capital has intensively poured into the freshly ground coffee market, especially low-priced specialty coffee priced at 15–25 yuan. Manner Coffee, a fresh brew coffee chain, only has 160 stores, and already supports a valuation of nearly USD $3 billion. Traditional retail formats that originally had many store asset advantages have also opened coffee businesses. For example, Sinopec's convenience store brand "Yi Jie", foreign fast food such as McDonald's and KFC have also added coffee areas in their stores, and foreign coffee brands such as Tim Hortons, a brand of coffee I grew up with in Canada, has also announced to open a thousand stores as soon as possible.

Shanghai is the city with the densest coffee shops in China. There are three to four coffee shops for every 10,000 people. The total number of coffee shops exceeds that of cities such as New York and London. Manner Coffee, another contender in the fresh coffee space currently has 90% of its stores located in Shanghai and are profitable.

In an ironic turn of events, Wu Jun now feels the need to return to offline. In August of this year, Saturn Bird Coffee will open its first official offline concept store on Anfu Road, Shanghai. After the offline store is established, Saturnbird Coffee will use the membership growth system as the core to connect online and offline customers, providing them with a rounded experience.

Formulating an Ecommerce Strategy in China

Now comes the fun part, where we are going to synthesize everything we've learned so far. From the core knowledge, to the theoretical concepts, to learning from the successes we have seen in China. What are the actual steps you need to do to set up ecommerce in China?

1. **Pick your product and research**

   Of course, before any project is to begin, we have to first research the market. There are many companies to hire for such an endeavor including my own firm. (Send me a message on Linkedin!) A study on the size of market, potential of revenue, current solutions in the market, competitive landscape are all basic items that are suggested to research.

2. **Craft your unique story**
   In Chinese, we call this 品牌定位 pǐn pái dìng wèi also known as the brand positioning. Now that you've known what is existing in the market, what makes your product special? Is it a certain function that a local player does not have? Is it the origin of the product? Is it the material or ingredient the product is made from? Basically, what makes the product unique in the market? I've seen many brands that are seemingly inexpensive in the home market, but because they had crossed over to China, they were positioned differently. For instance, Pizza Hut is a relatively mass brand in the US home market but was positioned as a high-end brand in China. (People go on dates in Pizza Hut China!) Or a brand like Tommy Hilfiger, a brand that has been having decreasing market share in the home market but was able to massively turn its brand around after heading into China.
3. **Set goals and milestones**
   Now that you know what makes you unique, what is the firm trying to achieve in the next year, the next three years, the next five and ten years? Is the company simply trying to enter the market to increase sales at home or is this market deemed a strategic market for the future of the brand? I have seen many brands wanting to enter the market without an actual goal in mind. To many, China seems to be a large market that is to be exploited, but how does this market's role play into the larger goals of the company?
4. **Set a budget for market entry**
   Is the brand going to enter online only or also offline? Is both going to be done at the same time? This will tie into how the brand is positioned to grow in the country and the goals that we had discussed earlier. If the brand is to only test the water via an ecommerce platform for instance, will one channel be enough? Perhaps it's wiser to set up shop in at least two different marketplaces.
5. **Find a solid partner or build your own team**
   If the budget is quite tight, the first step for most companies is to simply use a partner, either by way of a distributor or a TP. After the brand is more established in the market, the brand can then proceed to establishing an entity and hiring locally. It is also dependent on if the brand is viewing China as a long-term strategy. Some brands, for instance, have home markets that are extremely small. To grow to a global scale, they must tackle a large market like China to sustain

growth. In this case, it is wiser to consider building locally to have a more solid footing in the foreign market.

6. **Set the right communication strategy with the local market**

   This is something that many companies overlook, thinking that the default communication strategy in the home market is enough to be replicated in China. Instead, the main method for China to communicate in the working world is through Wechat (an app that was mentioned in Chapter 1) or Dingtalk (which is a communication app by Alibaba) Both apps function similarly to Slack in the west. Because just-in-time communication tools are preferred to discuss business matters, email is not as popular among Chinese companies, which also explains the rapid speed that decisions and projects are rolled out in China.

7. **Define KPI's and a way to measure results along the way**

   Depending on which method was chosen (whether distributor, TP or hiring a local team), it is important to provide the correct KPI's for the group for them to know what to deliver once the year is over. Meetings throughout the year is also needed as checkups to see what are the current small milestones reached.

8. **Review and adjust**

   Like the agile methodology and waterfall approach in product management, something similar is needed as you project-manage the journey in China, except in this case, you must measure and adjust in an even faster pace. Before I worked in China, I was in New York, a city with a pace that is considered quite rapid from a global perspective. After I arrived in China however, I realized that the New York pace can actually be quickened. We have a saying at Alibaba which is "one must learn how to change the airplane motor even in flight." What we are trying to say is many projects are not thought through in completion before it is launched. China truly embraces the concept of "failing fast". If something is not working, it is important to know to adjust quickly and try something else.

How to Work Best with the Platform

Having been previously a Category Manager in the platform, I've faced many different styles of working with brands and TPs. There is definitely no standard but there are some best practices which I will list below.

Do's

1. **Find your Category Manager**
   If you are a very large brand, most likely you will be paired with a merchant manager to aid you in the ecommerce process as their KPI's are tied to the success of your brand, the more you grow, the better this person will be compensated. However, if you are a smaller brand, you will more so rely on someone called the Category Manager. This role is responsible for growing an entire category within the platform, including what we call the "Long tail merchants". Add your category manager on Dingtalk or Wechat and try to maintain a close and personal relationship with them.
2. **Secure a meeting spot with them on a quarterly basis and before campaigns**
   Category Managers are very busy (think your brand multiplied by the number of brands they handle and sometimes this can be in the thousands) so it is very difficult to find time for them to meet. Usually though they will request a meeting with larger brands when it is a season before an S level campaign. For instance, 618 or Double 11.
3. **Lay out a brand's goals in a clearly defined PowerPoint**
   Usually this sort of PowerPoint will be made by the TP to be forwarded to a Xiaoer before the store is opened. But the more detailed this ppt is, the better. This is so the platform can get to know what type of brand this store will be and what to watch out for.
4. **Actively participate in campaigns**
   This is a great part about Chinese ecommerce compared to other geographies because these are platform-led campaigns which means the platform will have a huge incentive to have as much traffic into the app as possible. There will be platform provided coupons that brands can take advantage of that sets it apart from a normal daily campaign in which the brand is responsible for all discounts provided.
5. **Learn from the best**
   Category Managers will always be pushing out a ranking list of the top selling brands in the category as a "scoreboard". Thus, you will be able to see who is doing the best in the category. These

merchants will be told by the platform to do sharings of best practices, which are always useful to listen to. The merchant community is very different from one in the west where information is more siloed. Because there are also many merchant conferences throughout the year, a lot of information and resources are shared amongst competitors of the same category that is great for a new brand to learn.

6. **Trade resources**

   Look at the platform as a resource to you. For instance, are there special events such as certain marketing IP's that can be awarded to you as a brand? Do you fall into some of their categories such as a green product or socially good product? The platform is providing more and more rebates and investments in these areas that you can leverage.

7. **Join the category Dingtalk group and keep an eye out for resources provided by the platform**

   All categories have their own Dingtalk groups. Dingtalk is Alibaba's chosen tool to communicate to merchants. A Category or Merchant Manager will be communicating major news announcements and updates to the platform via this channel. A big mistake I have seen from other brands when participating in marketing IP's is the slowness of the brand to respond. Dedicate one digital person to be the person on the lookout for resources from the platform and relay this information as soon as possible to the headquarters of the brand.

Dont's

1. **No goal in mind**

   KPI's are always needed no matter which stage the store is, even if it is a small one in the beginning. It helps the team put their heads together toward something and is a good numerical measure for how well a brand can do in the future.

2. **Don't go in without a plan**

   Even if you are starting out, do have a plan in mind and a vision for how the Chinese market can do for your company overall. For some brands, China is a long term and strategic market because of the consumer population.

3. **Don't be afraid of experimentation**
   Because of the vast number of channels in China and types of brands, it is possible that main channels are not for you. So be open to trying new platforms and ways of advertising. Fortune favors those who are willing to experiment.
4. **Expect the platform to provide free resources**
   The platform is incentivized to take fast growing brands and make them even bigger. So initially, a brand must prove that it is worthy of such investment. By simply opening shop on the platform does not demonstrate that you are a brand worth extra resources from the platform. You must demonstrate with initial numbers that this is a good brand for the platform to grow with.

How to Choose TP's

I've spoken to many brands, large and small and have gathered a wealth of response on their opinions on TPs. While the west is slowly maturing in this market with the largest TP-like company being Pattern, a VC funded start up based out of Utah and other ecommerce accelerators such as Thrasio and Perch, the TP business in China was born much earlier.

According to the "China E-commerce Service Industry Development Report", in 2019, the number of domestic TP service providers reached 89,000, a year-on-year growth rate of 9.89%. There are thousands of smaller TPs within China, some, with one customer. On the other end, there are TP's that serve hundreds of customers, employing tens of thousands of people. Most have some sort of specialization in either fashion, supplements, or beauty. From the TP's side, once they have garnered a relationship also with the category manager from the platform, it is easier for them to secure spaces for advertising within the app. This is another reason why it is beneficial for TP's to concentrate on their category instead of expanding them.

Baozun

https://www.baozun.com/

The largest TP at time of writing is Baozun. It is publicly traded on the NASDAQ with the ticker BZUN and has a plethora of large brands as customer including Philips, Microsoft, Nike and many others.

Buy Quickly

https://www.buyquickly.com/en/

This TP has largely been entrenched in affordable luxury fashion. Its main roster of clients are SMCP, Theory, Triumph among others.

Qingmu

http://www.qingmudigital.com/

This TP is another more mass TP who has hosted famous brands such as H&M, Ecco, Stuart Weitzman and other global brands.

TP's are ranked by a star system, evaluated each year based on data efficiency, quality of service, size of brands managed and overall customer satisfaction. Tmall announced a list of star-level service providers for the first half of 2020. The list is a comprehensive evaluation of these TP service providers based on relevant data indicators. The assessment indicators include operation quality, service quantity, and revenue-generating value.

Tmall selected 486 starred service providers in its 2020 roundup. Among them, 12 are six-star service providers (with a threshold of over 1 billion cumulative transactions), 42 five-star service providers (with a transaction threshold of 500 million), 58 four-stars, 69 three-stars (threshold value of 100 million), and 485 one- and two-star service providers (threshold value of 10 million). Among the top ten, more than 80% of the companies are "resident" six-star TP service providers, and 20% are new entrants with high entry barriers, while the top three performers dominates 45% of e-commerce revenue performance, and its triumphal position in the past two years is still unshakable.

However, there are many other TP's that are smaller and possibly more responsive that brands like to use. Ultimately it is about the team that is taking care of your brand which is highly contextual and subjective. The star system is a good guide for a TP's full set of capabilities, but sometimes, if you are not a massive, global brand with 10,000 SKU's to manage, sometimes it is more value for money to hire a smaller boutique TP. It is, however, always good to hear out the other success cases that the TP has already handled.

TP Business Model

TP's will have three ways of working with the brand: having a monthly fee plus commission, purchasing outright and being a distributor, or acting on behalf of the brand and taken a commission based on the total sales.

Monthly service fee + commission:

This is perhaps the most common form of working with a TP. Because a TP needs to hire customer service managers, designers, and store managers to manage every single brand, they will most likely want a monthly service fee to cover these basic costs. A commission is then in place to incentivize the TP to manage the store in a way that will maximize sales.

Currently prices roughly range from 20,000 RMB to 100,000 RMB per month depending on the number of SKU's and experience level of the TP. Commission usually ranges from 8 to 20%. If you are a smaller brand, most likely the TP will negotiate a higher service fee and lower commission as the store is growing and accruing customers. If you are a larger brand, you can most likely negotiate to have a lower service fee and higher commission.

Purchasing directly:

This mode is usually best for the brand, when there is no more responsibility in the ecommerce side of things. You can argue that when a TP has higher confidence in the brand, they are willing to directly purchase. The ill side of this is all of the data gathered will belong to the TP, unless it is explicitly required by the brand to be relayed this information. Another disadvantage is the store can be fully owned by the TP in this case. If the brand, one day, wanted the store reigns to be returned, it is possible to run into the issue of needing to shut down the entire store and then re-opening again with the brand as the registering party. As a brand, if you are relying on the TP to open the store in a direct purchase model, it is best to make sure with your TP that the registering entity for the store is still you, the brand.

Pure Commission:

Very rarely will the TP ask for a pure commission model. This is also rather advantageous for the brand in that they are simply providing a cut of the sale to their service partner. All payments are decided according to the revenue generated. A TP in this case might negotiate on a tiered bonus structure. For instance if sales are 0–100,000 RMB, the commission is 5%. For every additional hundred thousand, one more per cent is raised. The TP in this case is incentivized in the right way to do well in sales, but very rarely will established TP's opt for this route. However, if you are a large brand, it is possible to negotiate a contract like this where the TP knows that a certain amount of sales is going to be guaranteed.

The Zero to One of the World's Largest Fashion Brand

H&M is a name not foreign to lovers of fashion. Its simplistic designs, affordable prices, and convenient locations easily carved out its market share globally in the past couple of years. It was the same case for H&M when it was looking to enter China. With a sprinkle of physical stores in China, Magnus Omstedt, then Head of Online Expansion was faced with a problem when considering Tmall. Similar to many brands as they face the platform conundrum, H&M had one question. To join or not to join? And if so, what does that look like?

At the time, when H&M entered China, apart from their 500 physical stores, they had an official online shop and a WeChat mini program. But since this was the first potential marketplace ever for H&M, they were initially reluctant. Magnus was clear about the need for a Tmall presence ever since he had joined the company but still consulted with both McKinsey and BCG before following their recommendation to launch on Tmall.

For a large company, an H&M opening on a marketplace was like "fitting a square into a circle". All IT integrations and necessary infrastructure needed to be adapted. Simple things such as supply chain, logistics, marketing, setup of a local team and accounting were all functions that needed to be reworked to meet platform requirements. For the Tmall launch, Magnus needed to setup a stream of cross functional projects within the overall roadmap to secure the launch.

From Ideation to Launch

The first meeting started with a formal presentation by the Tmall team in Sweden, with several main members of the Alibaba Europe team present. The full launch for China from ideation to launch took half a year, which is quite fast for large companies like H&M.

At the time, there were fake resellers on Taobao even when H&M China was already in existence with physical stores and using the logo.

He knew that this would scare the management to continue the green light. However, this would be common for the platform. In fact, a high volume for C2C sales would indicate to the brand that there was existing interest already from the consumers of the platform.

As the project grew in maturation, the H&M brand CEO flew out to China to Hangzhou. Magnus recalls the boardroom table was so large that no one could reach the other side of the table to shake hands. The PowerPoint on the screen showed some figures for Double 11, including competitor numbers. The Alibaba team had a proposal including what marketing support would be needed. He remembered the tone from the team as if the brand wasn't very important to Alibaba but given that H&M was the last fast fashion retailer to launch on the platform, he recognized this was just part of the negotiation.

Magnus recalls that some months after the launch when he was wandering around the Alibaba campus, he saw an internal branding poster inside the staff bathrooms boasting about the success of H&M on Tmall.

The H&M Management at the time was concerned about cannibalization of the brand because the advent of the Tmall store. They thought this would possibly eat away from the physical store. However, Tmall serves as a brand beamer across China; the Tmall launch drove more traffic into the physical stores, a prediction that Magnus knew was to happen. They later experimented with the idea to implement delivery fulfillment by the store, a practical move by many fashion brands.

After Tmall was successfully setup, H&M became much more positive to marketplaces in general and have since then launched on several other marketplaces in order to echo the success H&M garnered in China.

Things Take a Turn

In 2020, because of a notice announced by the PR team of H&M to no longer support the purchase of cotton from Xinjiang, Chinese netizens went on a furious rampage against the brand. Overnight, the post was circulated by millions of Chinese consumers vowing to boycott the brand. The Tmall store was closed by the government overnight. The Swedish group moreover shut down about 20 of its 500 outlets and have experienced a 25% decrease in sales.

Today, Magnus runs his own company called Tritanium Ventures, which seeks to bring smaller and more niche fashion brands to China. Like me, he also thinks these matters can be avoided. When I asked him what he would have done differently, he said "I would always ask the Chinese person at the table. Maybe they are not verbose like the Swede, but they will bring an important perspective."

I also asked if he was a brand today and were to enter the market, what three tenets would he stick to. "Do research. Focus on the brand. And the west is not the best."

"I would look at what brands are doing well, what trends are, and how to complement the difference. Are you unique? Use that to enter by branding. Do a seeding campaign. Be Subtle. You can launch a campaign with LRB, WeChat, influencers and use Tmall as sales platform. There are so many things in Tmall. Use Alimama to target the RIGHT visitors."

"In terms of e-commerce, the West is not best. You can learn a lot from China and how to engage the Chinese consumer and then apply this in the west. Trends are set in China, and can develop in the west. You have to be curious. But that's why it's fun."

China, a Strategic Market for Adidas

The year was 2009, the first Double 11 campaign for Tmall. Actually, at the time, it was called Taobao Mall. Only brands like Nine west and Jack Jones were on the platform. When the then senior leader in digital joined Adidas, who has chosen to remain anonymous for the purpose of this interview, he made a strategic move in Jan 2016. He got his foot in the door of the largest consumer market in the world. At the time, sales in China was an abysmal share of the total global market, and it wasn't because China wasn't performing; there were two people in his ecommerce team; the strategy on Tmall was to sell whatever was leftover from the discounted items from the physical stores; China was largely overlooked as a market. Fast forward just five years, the China business is the most profitable, and fastest growing. Its market share internally rivals that of Europe and the Americas.

Nike was one step ahead in 2015. Both firms worked with BCG which had directed both brands to Tmall. "To gain scale with what is out there, you have to work with platform," is what BCG had advised. But not many brands did this successfully. Nike invested heavily in its own ecosystem while Adidas went all in by choosing Tmall as a partner.

When Adidas joined, the initial strategy was to concentrate on new customer acquisition and then enjoy each customer's Lifetime Value. Unlike how other brands approached the platform, he didn't want to think of themselves as a discount platform. His first pain point was to set up a team: pick a vendor, hire a team and choose the right merchandise.

As with any product on the market, what differentiates you from just being a commodity is how you tell the story. "If you're not an Apple, what will you do to cause a line at your store?" In the next few years, he led with three key words: Premium, Personalized, and Connected.

Now the business is 25% online, 75% offline, but online represents most of influence. "If we boil it down, the point of digital is influence and sales," he said. "Consumers in stores look at offline, and then online. They look at reviews and user generated content. Imagine if that online piece was not there."

He predicts that every company in the durables market will have China as the most important market or at least in the Top 2 or 3 and that global brands will increasingly have product design and technology be hosted in China. A China Board member is probably something large brands need to consider. This is so that in case something happens geopolitically; China can still survive. "The walls might get bigger, which warrants a bifurcation of strategy. What happens in mainland and what happens out of mainland."

"A huge part of the future is about sustainability," he said. Soon, 80% of Adidas products will all be made from sustainable materials. Its supply chain has a goal of eliminating plastic. "It will be as important as digital was in 2010. Things rooted to purpose has a greater chance of survival."

We have already seen a change in trend in the Gen Z market in which carbon neutral is a concept they are ready to pay for. As someone who cares deeply about the environment, I also hope he is right.

Implications of Ecommerce on Society and Environment

Another way to look at ecommerce is simply an alternative way to look at retail and commerce in general, lending itself further into general trade. As the world increasingly embraces ecommerce, essentially, it is increasingly embracing trade and consumption. This, of course, has many implications on society from a socio-economic and environmental perspective.

Ecommerce's Impact on Chinese Society

As 986 million Chinese people are introduced to ecommerce, an equally large mass of people in China are affected from a social and economic standpoint. As new brands are created in China, local resources are used up, local factories churn out more jobs and consumers end up having more choices for purchases. Increased number of brands and players increase competition and aid the quality of products produced and increase innovation in each sector to fine tune competitive advantages.

Ecommerce has been spotlighted in a way to induce entrepreneurship and poverty alleviation. Livestreaming provides for a way for farmers to be able to show the rest of the country what farms look like, how fruits are produced, and provides for a connection between city-dwellers and rural inhabitants. Hundreds of types of new roles in the work force have been born due to ecommerce: everything from livestream hosts to store managers to ecommerce data analysts.

However, ecommerce has not been beneficial for everyone. Mom and pop corner stores and offline specialty stores that were opened by hard-working families have been forgotten in this retail evolution as consumers adopted digital. Those who are not digitally literate such as senior citizens and disabled people have also had a harder time adopting to these changes. I remember watching a video that had once gone viral on Douyin illustrating a seventy year old man walking to a supermarket to buy grapes and later detained by the police because he was unable to pay electronically and only had cash with him. The digital era has also left traditional cashiers and retail associates jobless. Traditional shopping malls are having less and less foot traffic and nears full closures. These spaces are beginning to evolve even in China's rural areas.

Ecommerce's Impact on Rural China

Jack chose rural China as one of his key strategic pillars and started the Rural Taobao model a few years ago in the format of Taobao villages.

I visited the Rural Taobao village of Ulanqab in Inner Mongolia where Taobao had chosen several offline locations to increase market share in the region in 2018. Physical locations like this were used as a central community center to help people in the village order things from Taobao. They were also used as a pickup locker when packages arrive. The digitally illiterate relied on the people in the Taobao shop to top up their cell phones, pay electricity bills, and buy basic goods such as clothing or furniture.

On my trip, I learned a word which was used to describe these types of places, the 993861 village. 99 described the senior citizens since in Chinese 99 means to live a long time; 38 described the women since March 8th is International Women's Day; 61 described the children since June 1st was China's Children's Day. This meant that the village was populated for the most of year by senior citizens, women and children since the young men were away working elsewhere as the breadwinner. Some of these shops extended into supermarkets, convenience stores, card-playing recreational centers, and places to babysit children. They essentially became community centers for those who were idle during the day. For the 560 million people living in rural areas, community centers like this acted as a strong pillar in their support system.

Photo taken at a Rural Taobao physical shop in Ulanqab, Inner Mongolia

Is Ecommerce Better for the Environment?

Perhaps a whole book can be written for this topic alone especially in the age of climate-sensitivity that we are in. China has already voiced its concern for the environment, after decades of rapid economic development which spurred massive investments in manufacturing. As the country transitions its economy to knowledge services, the Chinese government has also projected its short-term environmental goals—to reach peak emissions by the year 2030 and to be completely carbon neutral by 2060.

Overall, Oliver Wyman purports that ecommerce is good for the environment. "The environmental impact of e-commerce appears to be positive. Offline shopping results in between 1.5 and 2.9 times more greenhouse gas emissions than online shopping." Ecommerce calls for more delivery vans to make routes for delivery, but there is much more accumulation in routes versus single family cars making trips. Land use for e-commerce is lower than for physical retail when multiple physical locations have to be opened across the country.

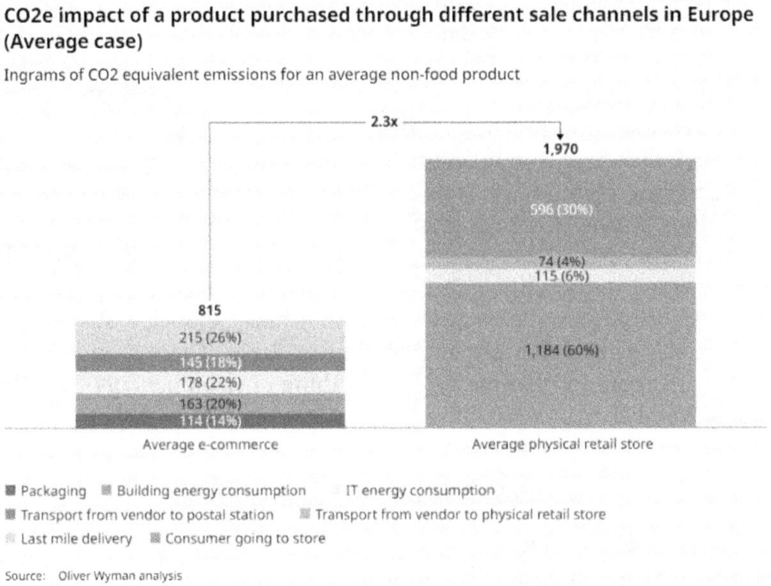

Oliver Wyman Ecommerce impact on environment report

The largest difference in emissions is in delivery. While brick and mortar stores have all of their customers coming to the brick and mortar location, the ecommerce division of the same store can have one route that covers all deliveries for its customers. Next, the amount of electricity needed to keep a store open even with little foot traffic can be wasteful versus the couple of servers that an ecommerce store would need. Finally, the amount of packaging that is generated from ecommerce needs to be made from sustainably sourced and biodegradable materials to lessen the burden on the environment. As consumers have a greater appetite for buying fresh products online, we will run into a bigger and bigger problem especially in cold chain products. When we were dealing with cold chain products in Tmall food, the packaging that was needed would double, since brands needed also dry ice and Styrofoam to keep the items cool until the product reached the customer. That has not even counted for the cold chain trucks that operate in different temperatures versus a normal truck.

My time in China in relation to sustainability has certainly differed far from my education in Canada. I remember we needed to calculate how many planets would be needed if everyone lived my lifestyle at around age ten. Students learned about recycling before they learned algebra (if you have never taken this test before, this is a great site to do it: footprintnetwork.org). However, sustainability in China is only starting to take shape. My Hangzhou community compound had only started recycling in 2020 so needless to say, China is quite far from reaching the same level of consumer concern as the west. However, when China wishes something to be enacted quickly, they also waste no time. Already, I'm beginning to see "carbon neutral" on packaging in China, and Gen Z opting to purchase things that they are reusable or recyclable. There is an imminent trend that is coming that indicates something environmentally-friendly is actually trendier than something that is not.

Tmall's Take on the Green Revolution

2021's year of Double 11 is the first year in which consumers can use vouchers for eco-friendly products and cartons will be recycled by the 60,000 Cainiao depots across China. Alibaba is also encouraging green shopping with a green marketplace, where shoppers can get green coupons and other deals for their shipping experience.

This Double 11 with the opening of a special campaign page dedicated to products that are of the same "green" trend, in the future, I do predict this will be the direction. I wouldn't be surprised if the Taobao product was later upgraded with a tab of information to include the CO_2 that a product is generating to influence consumers to purchase greener products. As with most things in China, if the government wishes to achieve something, it is sure that companies will adopt which will later affect consumers to adopt this trend as well.

Taobao screenshot of the 2021 D11 green marketplace

Beyond China

Congratulations you're almost at the end of the book! Thank you for staying with me until the end. Before we end our book though, I wanted to share some other pieces that would be useful for all the readers out there. China's advancements in ecommerce and retail will serve as a blueprint for further platforms around the world. Alibaba has, throughout the years, acquired and invested in various ecommerce platforms, in Southeast Asia, South Asia and Africa and is rapidly developing certain markets in Europe. Below are a few marketplaces though that brands will see a massive similarity to the Tmall in mainland.

Tmall HK

In Q4 of 2020, we began planning Tmall HK and we launched formally in May 2021. This is the first Tmall footprint outside of Chinese borders with local merchants and local delivery. There are four main product differentiations that make it different than the local apps, with the primary competitor being HKTV Mall.

1. 7 day return
2. Local delivery
3. Free logistics
4. Branded products

Taking part in this project allowed me to see how to build an ecommerce platform from scratch. From the market research done initially on the region, deciding which categories are the best to attract, which merchants to recruit, building certain product features, and developing a viable logistics plan, the project is an ever-evolving journey.

4:24
4G
天貓香港
跨境
本地
coach
抽濕
佐丹奴
7天無憂退貨 · 本地發貨 · 滿額免運 · 品牌好貨
每日爆品
服裝配飾
半價美妝
數碼家電
零食百貨
熱賣至抵買 限量搶券
SKII神仙水只售HK$807
立即搶購>
每日閃購
每朝10:00開搶
80% OFF
HK$120
55% OFF
HK$89
50% OFF
HK$19
基因修復精華
立減HK$50
補貼價$733
SK-II 護膚精華
立減HK$50
補貼價$807
在線 客服
SK-II 護膚面膜
立減HK$50
Dyson 吸塵機
立減HK$200
首頁
分類
購物車
我的

Lazada

Lazada grew its name from selling electronic goods mostly as a C2C marketplace. It has a similar platform image as Tmall HK with 100% Authenticity, 15-Day Easy Returns and Next Day Delivery. Lazada operated in a very similar way to Tmall: brands open a store on LazMall. One of the benefits of having a Tmall flagship store is being able to navigate the system.

Lazada is a B2C marketplace servicing 6 countries in South East Asia: Singapore, Malaysia, Indonesia, Thailand, Vietnam, and Philippines. Lazada offers both a domestic and cross-border model for merchants that may not have local entities, logistics and fulfilment capabilities in each market. Does that mean if you are already a Tmall brand, you can directly access Lazada and the southeast Asian market? Well, I'd say it is a lot easier for you, but it is not automatic, at least it's not at the time of writing. Brands do need to open another flagship store and then can copy paste products to their Lazada store, but Southeast Asia is poised to be the next region that will experience a spurt of growth in the next ten years. It is an excellent economy to invest in.

Lazmall Maybelline Flagship Store

Works Cited

Ai, K. (2021). 被罗永浩、吴晓波点赞的认养一头牛, 是如何年吸千万粉, 实现客单翻倍的 *How did the adoption of a cow praised by Luo Yonghao and Wu Xiaobo attract tens of millions of followers each year and double the customer order?* 36kr. Retrieved from: https://www.36kr.com/p/1442130188387972

Ap, T. (2021). *Neiwai launches sustainable capsule with Wolford*. WWD. Retrieved from: https://wwd.com/fashion-news/intimates/neiwai-launches-sustainable-capsule-with-wolford-1234953544/

Chenli, S., & Platonov, I. (2019). *Saturnbird Coffee, Nestlé Rival in China, raises tens of millions of Yuan*. Retrieved from: https://equalocean.com/analysis/2019112212236

Oliver Wyman. (2021). *Is ecommerce good for Europe*. Oliver Wyman. Retrieved from: https://www.oliverwyman.com/our-expertise/insights/2021/apr/is-e-commerce-good-for-europe.html

Omstedt, M. Interview. By Sharon Gai. 15 Nov 2021.

Tang, P. (2021). *21分钟爆卖1个亿背后, 自嗨锅的"营销陷阱" Behind the sales of 100 million yuan in 21 minutes, the "marketing trap" of Zihai Pot*. Sina Finance. Retrieved from: https://finance.sina.com.cn/tech/2021-08-03/doc-ikqcfncc0553565.shtml

Yun, Y. (2020). 三位80后校友敲钟: 完美日记正式IPO, 市值460亿 *Three post-80s alumni ring the bell: Perfect Diary's official IPO, with a market value of 46 billion*. PE Daily. Retrieved from: https://news.pedaily.cn/202011/462356.shtml

Zhou, V. (2021). What happened to Li Ziqi, China's most famous YouTuber? *Vice*. Retrieved from: https://www.vice.com/en/article/qj8qqv/li-ziqi-youtube-star-business-china

Epilogue

When I had first arrived in China, I was once told by someone if there were no goods travelling amongst borders, soldiers will. Suddenly that made my tireless 996 work cycle seem a bit more motivating. If I had a hand in stopping the third world war, I was all for it.

I do notice a difference in sentiment that runs contrary to the sentiment years ago. These days, when I'm at a Chinese dinner table in China, my relatives would ask *does everyone in America own a gun? Why are Covid cases so high, are they not able to control their own people?* And when I'm at a dinner with Americans, they too often ask, *don't you feel restrained in China? Are people happy there?* When I say yes, they continue to press, *but how can they be, with all the restrictions and lack of freedom?* I am forever caught in the middle of trying to bring both sides to understand the other a bit better.

China is like a misunderstood animal, a little lost in how to explain itself, because it is so unique and complicated. I do hope that the western view towards China rises beyond Kung-Fu, copycats, and its political system because there is so much more underneath the surface.

In this century, China experiments unendingly and has a vengeful ambition for growth. Quieted by the years of the Opium War, China later saw the economic reform by Deng Xiao Ping as salvation. Now that the American Dream has made splashes across global headlines, the Chinese Dream seeks to replicate something similar. However, a big difference is things will not be allowed done with absolute self-guided direction. There

S. Gai, *Ecommerce Reimagined*,
https://doi.org/10.1007/978-981-19-0003-7

is an invisible hand that will guide these entrepreneurial forces. After all, it is this central coordination that enables the country to grow at the speed it does today.

If I can pinpoint one thing China is exceptional at, it's coordination. The ability to herd a thousand or a million different actors in one direction holds immense power to the footprint this group can have on the world. Technically, movements like this are happening everywhere around the world. But in China, these movements happen fast and are thoughtfully curated with many long-term plans in place. And it is this timely coordination that is what I think will make China a most unique place in the future.

As an employee of a company that has bled orange, I myself have endured similar things. And as someone who had grown up in a western world, I had my fair share of adjustments. Perhaps for my next tome, I will tell the world about stories while working at Alibaba. (If you are interested, please let me know via my socials!) I would concentrate more heavily on the difference in culture to highlight these difficulties that the two worlds present. And maybe, between the final lines, I can harbor the insight to find out how to make these two players work with each other.

If any of the stories or information has been useful for you, please reach out and let me know. I read all your messages and emails. Linkedin is an easy channel for me. I'd love to hear about what you think of the content and what I should write next!

Until next time.

Index

S. Gai, *Ecommerce Reimagined*,
https://doi.org/10.1007/978-981-19-0003-7

Printed in the USA
CPSIA information can be obtained
at www.ICGtesting.com
LVHW010428241223
767241LV00007B/670